COMPREHENSIVE GUIDE TO BLENDED FAMILY SUCCESS

Essential Strategies for Smooth Transitions, Mastering Co-Parenting, and Creating a Cohesive, Joyful Home

---

TAYLOR REED

© Copyright Taylor Reed 2024 - All rights reserved.

The content within this book may not be reproduced, duplicated or transmitted without direct written permission from the author or the publisher.

Under no circumstances will any blame or legal responsibility be held against the publisher or author for any damages, reparation, or monetary loss due to the information contained within this book. Either directly or indirectly. You are responsible for your own choices, actions, and results.

Legal Notice:

This book is copyright-protected and only for personal use. You cannot amend, distribute, sell, use, quote, or paraphrase any part of the content without the consent of the author or publisher.

Disclaimer Notice:

Please note that the information in this document is for educational and entertainment purposes only. All effort has been expended to present accurate, up-to-date, reliable, and complete information. No warranties of any kind are declared or implied. Readers acknowledge that the author does not render legal, financial, medical, or professional advice. The content within this book has been derived from various sources. Please consult a licensed professional before attempting any techniques outlined in this book.

By reading this document, the reader agrees that the author is under no circumstances responsible for any direct or indirect losses incurred from using the information contained within this document, including, but not limited to, errors, omissions, or inaccuracies.

Contents

Introduction 7

1. **UNDERSTANDING THE BLENDED FAMILY DYNAMIC** 11
   Setting the Stage: Recognizing Your Blended Family's Unique Structure 11
   Communication: The Lifeline for Blended Families 16
   Creating a Shared Vision for Your Blended Family 19

2. **EFFECTIVE COMMUNICATION STRATEGIES** 23
   The Art of Active Listening in a Blended Family 23
   Transparency with Children and Teens 26
   Bonding Activities for Better Communication 28
   Handling Sensitive Topics Gracefully 30
   Family Meetings: A Tool for Democratic Household Management 32

3. **BLENDING PARENTING STYLES: CRAFTING HARMONY FROM DIVERSITY** 37
   Understanding Each Other's Parenting Styles 37
   Discipline in Blended Families: A Balanced Approach 40
   Handling Backlash: When Kids Challenge Unified Fronts 43

4. **MANAGING RELATIONSHIPS WITH EX-PARTNERS AND EXTENDED FAMILY** 47
   Co-Parenting with Ex-Partners: Keeping Kids First 47
   Navigating Extended Family Dynamics in Blended Families 49
   Holidays and Special Occasions: Planning for Success 51
   Setting Boundaries with Ex-Partners and Extended Family 54
   The Role of the Ex-Partner in Your Blended Family 56

5. FINANCIAL HARMONY IN BLENDED FAMILIES — 61
   - Combining Finances: A Step-by-Step Guide — 61
   - Child Support and Alimony: Navigating the Legal Landscape — 64
   - Saving for the Future: Education, Emergencies and Retirement — 66
   - Daily Financial Management in a Blended Family — 68

6. INTEGRATING CHILDREN AND TEENS INTO THE BLENDED FAMILY — 75
   - Understanding How Kids Feel in a Blended Family — 75
   - Strengthening Individual Family Bonds — 79

7. BUILDING A UNIFIED FAMILY CULTURE — 85
   - Establishing New Family Traditions That Honor All Members — 85
   - The Power of Family Rituals in Building Identity — 87
   - The Importance of Flexibility in Family Life — 90
   - Blending Family Histories: Sharing Stories — 92

8. TRANSFORMING BLENDED FAMILY DYNAMICS — 97
   - Strategies for Inclusion — 97
   - Managing Ex-Partner Relations: Building Cooperation — 99
   - Financial Planning: Creating a Plan for Everyone — 102

9. INTEGRATING INTO THE BLENDED FAMILY — 109
   - Finding Your Place in the Blended Family — 109
   - Managing Money Together: A Guide to Financial Unity — 112

10. BLENDED FAMILY STRATEGIES: EVERYDAY SOLUTIONS — 119
    - Tailored Solutions for Real-Life Challenges — 119
    - Interactive Tools for Active Problem-Solving — 121
    - Empowering Children and Teens — 123
    - Expert Insights: Professional Advice and Strategies — 125
    - Blended Family Successes: Inspirational Stories — 128

11. NURTURING HOPE AND RESILIENCE IN
   BLENDED FAMILIES   131
   Hope as a Foundation   131
   From Surviving to Thriving: Enhancing Family
   Dynamics   133
   Implementing Change: Steps for Immediate Results   136
   Strengthening Family Connections   138

   Conclusion   141
   References   145

Introduction

Let's kick things off with a little story—think of it as a glimpse into the gloriously messy world of blended families. There was once a dinner table, not unlike your own, around which sat a patchwork of individuals: a stepmom trying to decode the sullen teenager's grunts, a dad doing the awkward shuffle between his kids and his new partner's kids, and a couple of step-siblings engaging in a silent battle of wills over the last piece of pizza. This scene, my friends, is the perfect tableau of the beautiful chaos of a blended family. It's a mix of love, frustration, awkwardness, and deep connection that can only come from weathering life's storms together.

Hi, I'm the author of this little survival guide you're holding, and if that dinner table scenario had you nodding along or chuckling in recognition, you're exactly who I wrote this book for. My journey through the world of blended families, whether personal or through years of professional engagement, has shown me both the highs and the lows—the unique challenges and the extraordinary moments of joy. From this place of deep empathy and understanding, I've poured everything into creating a guide that's not just about surviving but thriving in your blended family.

Whether you're a remarried adult, a stepparent, or a child dealing with the ups and downs of blended family life, this book gives you practical advice, emotional support, and expert insights to make things easier. I've created this guide as a helpful resource you can turn to, no matter the challenge.

Our family structures may look slightly different, but the goals are the same: love, understanding, and harmony. This book is for all of you—remarried or re-partnered adults, stepparents, young children, and teenagers. It's an inclusive guide, addressing your unique needs and challenges with an empathetic, hopeful, and even a bit authoritative tone. Because let's face it, navigating blended family life without a sense of humor is like trying to assemble IKEA furniture without the instructions—possible, but why make it harder on yourself?

This book is divided into four parts that mirror your journey and are structured to guide you through the foundational aspects of building a blended family, tackling the inevitable challenges, managing the nitty-gritty of finances, and fostering growth. What sets this guide apart? It has personalized solutions and interactive elements to engage every family member. It focuses on the oft-overlooked perspectives of children and teens, expert insights, and inspirational stories from those who've walked this path and come out smiling.

So, consider this your invitation to dive in, apply the advice, and let this book be a companion on your journey toward building a harmonious blended family. Approach it with an open heart, a willingness to laugh at the messy moments, and a readiness to grow and learn together.

As we embark on this journey together, let me leave you with this note of hope: I believe in blended families' resilience and boundless potential to survive and thrive. With all its unique quirks and complexities, your family has everything it needs to write its own story of love and triumph. Let's get started, shall we?

ONE

Understanding the Blended Family Dynamic

Blended families are unique because they bring together different backgrounds and experiences, making family life complex and interesting. Each member has their own story of love, challenges, and growth. What makes these families unique isn't that they're perfect but how they fit all these pieces together to form a strong, vibrant family unit. Creating a blended family involves combining different lives and histories, which can be challenging. But it's by working through these challenges, that blended families find their way and become stronger together.

Setting the Stage: Recognizing Your Blended Family's Unique Structure

Diversity as Strength

Blended families are more than just a mix of different cultures or ethnicities; they include various experiences, personalities, and pasts. Each person brings their own life story, full of chapters, before they all come together. In these families, diversity is a source of strength rather than a barrier. It brings together different viewpoints, skills, and coping methods to help the family bond and understand each other better. For instance, a child asking about a tradition from their old home can lead to everyone sharing and learning about each other's backgrounds, which helps build connections.

The impact of this diversity is significant. Take a family where both parents have gone through their tough times, like loss or personal growth. These experiences can make them more empathetic, patient, and appreciative of happy moments together. While adjusting to new settings, their kids bring in new ideas and energy that add to the family vibe. This mix of different backgrounds and life stories creates a strong family unit that can handle challenges better together than individually.

Understanding Dynamics

Blended families are as diverse as the people in them, and there's no one way to describe how they work. It's essential to recognize that every family member brings something different and that variety can help the family thrive. Like how different flowers improve a garden, each family member adds value. Giving everyone their own space and understanding their unique role can create a peaceful atmosphere where everyone's needs are met.

This approach is essential when dealing with the roles of biological parents and stepparents. The relationships here can be complex, needing a mix of authority and understanding, guidance and freedom. It's all about finding a good balance in co-parenting that respects the existing family ties and the new ones made by stepparents. Keeping the lines of communication open, respecting each other, and focusing on what's best for the kids helps these relationships flourish.

Navigating Challenges

Blended families naturally face many challenges, from practical stuff like juggling schedules and household duties to deeper emotional issues like dealing with feelings of loss or figuring out where everyone fits. The trick to handling these challenges is to see them not as roadblocks but as chances to grow closer and strengthen the family bond.

For example, figuring out how to sync calendars between different households can be tough, but it also pushes everyone to devise creative ways to work together and communicate better. It's a chance to involve kids in making decisions, helping them feel valued and responsible. Likewise, tackling emotional issues head-on can increase empathy and understanding among family members, setting the stage for stronger, more genuine relationships.

Celebrating Uniqueness

At the core of successful blended families is valuing each member for who they are. This means actively appreciating everyone's different backgrounds, stories, dreams, and even the quirky stuff. It's all about building a family culture where these differences aren't just tolerated but truly valued.

This kind of celebration can look different for every family. It might mean blending elements from each person's cultural or religious background into your family traditions or making a big deal of everyone's achievements and milestones. The goal is to create an environment where everyone feels noticed, listened to, and appreciated for their true selves. This approach builds a strong sense of belonging and turns the family's diversity into a real strength.

By embracing blended families' unique makeup, seeing diversity as an asset, understanding the complex dynamics involved, handling challenges with determination, and celebrating each individual, blended family life can be fulfilling. They can set an example of love, unity, and resilience, showing that although blending a family requires patience, empathy, and understanding, the result is gratifying.

Embracing Diversity: Integrating Different Cultures and Traditions

Blended families combine cultures and traditions, which can be challenging but offer many growth opportunities. The secret to making it work is to respectfully integrate these diverse elements, turning what could be sources of conflict into reasons to celebrate together.

It all starts with open conversations fueled by curiosity. This dialogue helps everyone understand the stories and values behind each other's traditions, creating a bridge between people from different backgrounds. Learning about each other's cultures isn't just informative—it's a shared journey that can bring everyone closer.

Creating new traditions that respect everyone's backgrounds is like building a new family identity. It involves keeping some old traditions while introducing new ones that everyone in the family can call their own. This balance is key and requires everyone's input, which helps build a sense of shared ownership and pride.

Respecting each family member's background is crucial. This goes beyond accepting differences—truly appreciating what each person brings to the family. Simple gestures, like making a meal from someone's culture or incorporating elements of different religious practices into family celebrations, can make everyone feel valued.

Inclusive decision-making is vital for a blended family. This means everyone should be heard when deciding which traditions to keep and how to celebrate special occasions. This democratic approach helps strengthen family bonds and teaches everyone the value of respect and equity.

In practice, each family gathering is a chance to celebrate the family's diverse makeup. Holidays and everyday rituals offer opportunities to blend different cultural elements, from food to activities, creating a unique family culture that acknowledges everyone's heritage.

Integrating diverse cultures in a blended family ultimately leads to love and commitment. It's about building a life together that respects each person's past while creating a new, shared future. Through open communication, new traditions, respecting individual backgrounds, and inclusive decision-making, blended families strengthen their connections and show how diversity can lead to unity and enrichment.

The Role of Love: More Than Just a Feeling in Blended Families

Blending families means putting love into action. It's about doing the daily work and showing up for each other, not just feeling affection. This kind of active love forms the foundation of a blended family, turning every small gesture and compromise into a building block for a strong, loving home.

Building strong relationships in a blended family requires empathy and patience. These connections start fragile and can easily be strained by adjustments and tensions. However, they can grow into a strong, supportive network with enough care. Shared experiences are key. Whether cooking a meal together or celebrating a stepchild's achievements as enthusiastically as you would for your child, these moments bring everyone closer and create genuine, heartfelt joy.

Love also acts as a buffer against conflicts that naturally arise in families. Disagreements aren't just problems; they're chances to show how resilient love can be. Handling conflicts with a mindset that chooses love actively can turn these potential clashes into moments of understanding. Listening to each other's viewpoints shows respect and builds a family culture where differences are accepted and appreciated, helping everyone grow closer.

Reaffirming love and commitment is crucial in blended families. This goes beyond saying, "I love you." It shows up in everyday actions—recognizing each person's needs, sharing responsibilities, and supporting each other quietly but consistently. These actions ensure everyone feels valued and essential to the family's story.

Moreover, committing to face challenges together is vital, whether standing united during tough times or seeking help when family dynamics get too complicated. Being open to change and growth individually and as a family shows a readiness to adapt and mature together.

Ultimately, in a blended family, love is more than just affection. It's a conscious choice that shapes every interaction and decision. It acknowledges the complexities of merging lives and histories and provides a framework for building lasting, fulfilling relationships. In this context, love isn't just felt; it's the act of being a family.

Communication: The Lifeline for Blended Families

Good communication is key in blended families. It's not just about talking; it's about connecting, which means paying attention to what's said and what isn't. Listening is just as crucial as speaking. By truly understanding each other, you show your love and build stronger bonds. This helps everyone navigate misunderstandings and fosters a family environment filled with respect and affection.

Open Dialogue

Effective communication in a blended family hinges on keeping an open dialogue. The living room often becomes where everyone can speak their mind. It's where a teenager might slowly open up, encouraged by a caring stepparent, and a biological parent can express their concerns without fear of being judged. It's also a place where every win, big or small, is genuinely celebrated. The goal is to foster a transparent atmosphere where it's okay to ask questions and everyone's opinion is heard. This kind of open communication helps clear up any misunderstandings and strengthens the family's bond.

Active Listening Skills

Active listening is a key part of communication in blended families, though it often doesn't get the spotlight it deserves. It's more than just hearing words; it's about engaging with what's being said. This means paying full attention to the speaker, showing you understand their message, and remembering what's been shared. It's how a stepparent can pick up on a child's hidden need for acceptance in a simple shrug or how a biological parent can appreciate the real effort behind a partner's clumsy attempt at setting rules. When everyone in the family practices active listening, it builds trust, prevents small misunderstandings from blowing up into big fights, and makes everyone feel truly heard and valued.

Navigating Difficult Conversations

Navigating difficult conversations is a big part of life in a blended family. How you handle these talks can make all the difference. It's key to start by recognizing that being open about your feelings isn't a sign of weakness; it helps build stronger connections. When it comes time to discuss tough issues, whether it's clashing parenting styles, feeling left out, or dealing with ex-partners, the setting and approach matter a lot. You need a place without distractions where everyone feels comfortable to speak up and be heard. How you talk is important, too—keeping things calm and avoiding an aggressive tone can encourage openness instead of defensiveness. Techniques like using "I" statements to express feelings without blaming others, focusing on finding solutions, and setting clear, respectful boundaries can help turn potentially tense conversations into chances for the family to grow closer, heal, and strengthen their ties.

Regular Family Check-Ins

Blended families are constantly changing, with new challenges and evolving relationships. That's why it's so helpful to have regular family check-ins. Think of these as casual get-togethers, maybe around the dinner table or in the living room after eating, where everyone can catch up. These meetings are more than just time to review what everyone's schedule looks like; they're crucial for maintaining a strong family bond. They provide a space to discuss issues, celebrate successes, and adjust to whatever's new in everyone's lives. These gatherings are vital—they keep the family connected, ensuring everyone feels part of the group, and sharing laughs and sometimes even tears.

Communication is key in blended families—it keeps everything moving smoothly. Everyone can be heard by talking things out, building trust through active listening and carefully handling challenging conversations. Regular family check-ins celebrate where you've been and where you're heading, helping to strengthen relationships amidst the complexities of family life. It's this ongoing conversation that helps a blended family not just survive but thrive.

Building Trust from the Ground Up

In blended families, trust isn't just handed out; it's something you have to work on and earn through consistent and transparent actions. From the start, trust is fragile, but it can grow stronger through clear and open communication, where people don't just make promises—they keep them, and their actions match their words. This helps everyone feel more secure and like they truly belong.

Building trust hinges on consistency. Take a stepparent who promises to attend a stepchild's soccer game. Keeping that promise might seem small, but it's a huge step in building a solid relationship. Over time, these small actions add up, creating a dependable pattern everyone can count on. This consistency helps soothe the uncertainties often accompanying adjusting to a new family setup.

Of course, the journey to build trust isn't always smooth. Mistakes happen—misunderstandings or letdowns that can damage trust.

How you handle these bumps is crucial. Being transparent about the mistake, genuinely apologizing, and showing seriousness about fixing things can slowly mend the trust. It's about facing challenging issues directly, listening to the hurt you've caused, and showing through your actions that you're committed to making things right.

It's also important to celebrate when you reach trust milestones, like the first time a child confides in a stepparent or when everyone agrees on a family decision, trusting each other's intentions. Recognizing these moments, maybe with a family tradition or a simple thank you, can reinforce the trust you've built and encourage more of it.

Ultimately, every step you take with integrity, every promise you keep, and every milestone you celebrate strengthens the trust within the family. This trust becomes the foundation of your family's story, filled with shared experiences and deeper connections.

Creating a Shared Vision for Your Blended Family

In a home where different lives and stories come together, having a shared vision helps guide a blended family. This vision, created and cared for by everyone in the family, becomes more than just a goal—it becomes the family's core. It's made up of everyone's hopes, dreams, and values, and it helps steer the family through daily ups and downs and the more significant changes in relationships.

Visionary Planning

Planning for the future in a blended family means finding a good mix between what everyone individually wants and what's best for the group. This often starts with casual conversations, maybe over breakfast in a sunny kitchen or the living room as the evening sets in, where everyone can openly discuss their hopes and support each other's dreams. Parents and kids act like architects in these chats, sketching out what they hope the future will look like. They're building a plan that includes common goals and respects each person's wishes. Through these discussions, a clear and shared vision starts to form. This could be about creating a nurturing home, focusing on education, or celebrating both the significant achievements and the small victories. This shared vision then serves as a guiding light for the family, helping them navigate the path ahead.

Setting Collective Goals

Setting collective goals is crucial in making a family's shared vision come to life. These goals, which everyone in the family agrees on, act like concrete milestones that help bring the vision into reality. They can be simple and practical, like starting a weekly family night to boost connection and communication, or more ambitious, like organizing a family trip that celebrates the different cultures in the family. The important thing is to make sure these goals include everyone's ideas and needs. It's a team effort where kids and adults have equal say, ensuring everyone's views help shape the family's goals. This way, the whole family has a stake in setting and achieving these goals, enriching the journey together.

Adjusting and Evolving

Like anything alive and growing, a blended family keeps changing over time. While having a shared vision to guide you is great, staying flexible and adjusting to these changes is essential. As kids grow up and parents face new life phases, the family's goals might need to shift. This isn't a setback; it's just part of being resilient and ready to adapt to whatever comes your way. It's crucial to have regular check-ins where you all can pause and see if you're still on track with your core values and long-term goals. Keeping the lines of communication open is essential in this process. It helps keep the family together, ensuring everyone's on the same page even as things evolve.

Celebrating Achievements Together

The milestones a family reaches aren't just markers of progress; they're also times to celebrate the journey. Whether reaching a shared goal or overcoming a tough challenge, these moments are perfect for strengthening the family bond. Celebrating can be as simple as having dinner together or as big as throwing a party. These celebrations remind everyone of the strength they have together and the joy of succeeding as a team. They help the family reflect on their achievements and what's still ahead. Every success, big or small, shows the resilience, love, and commitment central to the blended family experience.

The family finds its groove, where everyone's paths unite harmoniously by creating and living out a shared vision. This vision guides their decisions, handling challenges and planning celebrations, giving everyday life a purpose and direction. It's a dynamic force shaped by everyone in the family, proving great strength in their unity despite their differences. By planning together, setting goals, staying flexible, and celebrating their wins, the family builds a future filled with support and love and takes concrete steps to make it happen.

TWO

Effective Communication Strategies

In family life, where everyone has a role and personality, communication is like the leader who keeps everything running smoothly. It sets the pace for how everyone gets along daily, helps people feel free to express themselves, and keeps everyone on the same page. Good communication is key in a blended family, where things can get pretty complex. It helps everyone understand each other better, clears misunderstandings, and builds a strong foundation of respect and love.

The Art of Active Listening in a Blended Family

Active listening is fully attending to one another, a skill that can transform relationships when practiced within the walls of a home. It's the difference between hearing and truly understanding, reacting and responding. Active listening fosters an environment where each family member feels valued and understood, laying the groundwork for trust and openness.

Foundations of Active Listening

Active listening involves three main things: paying full attention, showing you're listening, and giving feedback. This means putting away distractions, focusing entirely on the person talking, and using nods or saying things like "I see" to show you're engaged. It's an active process where you need to tune into not just the words but also the feelings and the things not being said. In a blended family, where it's easy for misunderstandings to pop up due to everyone's different backgrounds, getting good at active listening is crucial. It helps everyone feel understood and safe, smoothing potential bumps in family life.

Practical Listening Exercises

Try exercises to improve your active listening skills within the family. For example, during family meetings, have a time when each person can talk about their day while the others focus on listening to what's said and how it's felt. This simple activity helps everyone practice paying attention and understanding each other better, which can deepen the connections between everyone in the family.

Overcoming Barriers to Listening

In blended families, listening can sometimes be tripped up by assumptions, distractions, and emotional hang-ups. For example, a stepparent might not fully listen to a stepchild, thinking their concerns are typical teenage drama. Or a child might find it hard to listen to a new parent because they feel loyal to their biological parent. The first step to getting past these issues is to recognize them. Then, you can work on strategies like putting personal biases aside, ensuring conversations happen without distractions, and keeping an open and curious attitude. These steps can improve how well everyone listens to each other, strengthening family bonds.

Listening to Conflict Resolution

During a conflict, active listening can be a game changer, helping to cool things down and clear up misunderstandings. It brings out the real issues, making it easier to find solutions. When arguments pop up, try a listening-first method where everyone shares their side without interruption. This change in approach can make the situation feel less like a battle and more like a team effort. It emphasizes understanding each other rather than trying to "win" the argument, turning challenging moments into chances for everyone to grow closer and understand each other better.

Active listening is key to smooth communication in a blended family. It takes patience, effort, and a real commitment to see things from each other's viewpoints. By practicing this, misunderstandings can become moments for gaining new insights, and the family's different perspectives can unite into a unified expression of shared values and love.

Conflict Resolution: Strategies for Peaceful Problem-Solving

Conflicts are just a part of life in a blended family. They can be tense, but if handled with care, they also offer chances to grow and better understand each other. The first step is figuring out where these conflicts are coming from, which requires deep thinking and paying close attention to family interactions. It's about looking beneath the surface to find the real issues, whether unspoken expectations, blurred boundaries, or adjusting to new roles.

Once you know what's causing the conflict, it's time to work on solving it. The goal is to focus on constructive conversation rather than just butting heads. Using "I" statements helps express feelings without blaming others and sets the stage for open, defensive-free discussions. Setting specific times to discuss issues can also help, as it separates the immediate emotions from the solution-finding process. This approach can make conflicts less daunting and more like opportunities to strengthen family ties.

Sometimes, though, conflicts are too tough to handle alone. Bringing in someone neutral, like a respected family member or a professional mediator, can make a big difference. They can help everyone see the situation differently and find common ground.

Preventing conflicts is also crucial. This means setting clear expectations right from the start about everyone's roles and responsibilities, which helps avoid misunderstandings. Promoting a culture where everyone feels comfortable sharing their feelings regularly, not just when things go wrong, also helps nip potential problems.

By understanding what causes conflicts, managing them constructively, using mediation when needed, and taking steps to prevent them, blended families can turn challenging moments into chances for coming together. This approach doesn't just help avoid disputes; it builds a stronger, more connected family.

Transparency with Children and Teens

Age-Appropriate Transparency

When talking with kids and teens in blended families, it's essential to consider each child's age and maturity level to ensure you're being clear but not overwhelming them. Just like you wouldn't overload a small plant with too much water, you want to avoid burdening a child with more information than they can handle. Being honest is key, but you need to adjust the details to fit their ability to understand. For example, you could tell a younger child that the family needs to watch its spending, while you could go into more detail about budgeting and finances with a teen. This way of tailoring your transparency helps build trust and prepares kids and teens to handle life's challenges with more confidence and awareness.

Building Trust Through Honesty

In a blended family, trust is everything, and it's built on being honest consistently. When dealing with kids and teens, being honest means more than just not lying. It involves openly sharing what's happening in the family, including any challenges with blending lives. Sticking to this kind of honesty helps create a strong foundation of trust. This reduces the anxiety and pushback when kids feel unsure or left out of the loop. When children know they can count on their parents or stepparents to be honest, even about tough stuff, it gives them a sense of security that helps them navigate the complexities of growing up in a blended family. This kind of trust doesn't just strengthen individual relationships; it ties the whole family closer, making the family more united and resilient.

Involving Children in Family Discussions

Including kids and teens in family discussions shows them they're important family members. When invited to share their thoughts on where to go on vacation, what the house rules should be, or how to handle changes at home, it gives them a real sense of involvement and belonging. This is huge for their emotional and psychological growth. Valuing their opinions not only makes them feel respected but it also teaches them about responsibility and teamwork. They learn to work together, respect different views, and understand the importance of contributing to the family's well-being. This approach turns the family into a place where everyone's input is valued, building a strong foundation of mutual respect and shared responsibility.

Handling Sensitive Topics

Talking about tough topics in a blended family needs a careful mix of understanding and clear communication. It's all about respecting how sensitive these issues can be for kids and teens and giving them the right support to handle them. This means setting up a safe space where they can share any worries, confusion, or upset without fear of being judged and where they can ask questions and get honest, considerate answers.

Whether it's about a biological parent moving out, changes in who they're living with, or welcoming new family members, the way to handle these discussions should always focus on seeing things from the child's point of view, being patient with their questions, and helping them manage their feelings. Handling these sensitive topics well helps kids grow up emotionally healthy and builds up the trust and security they feel within the family, showing them that their family is committed to facing life's challenges together with openness and care.

Bonding Activities for Better Communication

In a blended family, where everyone has their unique personality and background, simply living together isn't enough to create harmony. Building shared experiences that help everyone connect and communicate better is crucial. Choosing and doing bonding activities together is a key part of this. These activities should be picked with everyone's interests in mind so they feel meaningful to each family member. Choosing the right activities can help strengthen the connections between everyone, bringing you closer together as a family.

Planning Inclusive Activities

Creating family activities that include everyone's interests ensures each family member feels represented. It starts with a good, open conversation where everyone gets to put their ideas on the table and take every suggestion seriously. Whether planning an exciting family adventure day or a calm afternoon doing art together, there are loads of options that can match the different interests of your family. The trick is to mix it up—rotate through activities so everyone's interests get a spotlight at different times. This way, everyone feels like they belong and can share a bit of their world with the rest. It's a great way to build empathy and understanding as you all experience and enjoy things together.

The Role of Play

Playing together has a special way of breaking down walls and showing how much we have in common. Whether laughing over a board game or teaming up for a sport, these moments unite everyone in the quest for fun and relaxation. Play is like a universal language everyone can speak, regardless of age, background, or role in the family. It sparks creativity and lets everyone's personality shine, helping to build stronger connections. More than that, playing together helps open up lines of communication. When everyone's having fun, it's easier to let your guard down, making room for building deeper relationships without even needing words. These play times add fun and togetherness to your family's story, creating a strong sense of unity that sticks around.

Regular Family Meetings

Holding regular family meetings shows how much everyone's input is valued. These meetings are a mix of structure and flexibility, providing a space where everyone can discuss things, support each other, and tackle problems together. There's usually a clear agenda to keep things on track, covering everything from concerns people might have to planning fun activities to celebrating what everyone's achieved. It doesn't matter how old you are; everyone can speak their mind in these meetings. This fair approach helps improve communication and brings everyone together, making the family feel more united and purposeful. These meetings aren't just about staying organized—they're key moments where the family bonds, reflects on things, and plans for the future, all of which keep the family's rhythm going strong.

Creating a Family Communication Charter

Creating a family communication charter is a cool way to make sure everyone in a blended family communicates well. This charter, which everyone helps make, is like a commitment to always talk openly, respectfully, and supportively with each other. It includes key rules like listening actively, using "I" statements to talk about feelings, and keeping conversations non-judgmental. It also lays out how to handle any issues or conflicts, making sure that when problems arise, everyone works together to solve them constructively. This charter isn't set in stone; the family can update it as things change, ensuring it always works for them. More than just rules, it represents the respect and values everyone shares, guiding everyone through the challenges of blended family life.

Choosing and doing bonding activities wisely is crucial for harmony in a blended family. All these elements are the foundation of family unity, from ensuring everyone's interests are considered when planning activities to playing together, from regular family meetings to following the communication charter. Through these efforts and shared commitments, the family can blend everyone's individuality into a beautiful and lasting harmony of communication, connection, and mutual respect.

Handling Sensitive Topics Gracefully

Approaching Difficult Conversations

Starting a conversation about touchy topics needs careful planning, much like figuring out the best path through a tricky situation. First, you must pick the right time to talk when everyone involved is calm and open to discussion. This way, the conversation starts on solid ground, focused on being receptive rather than reactive.

Next, you prepare by reflecting on what you want to achieve and gathering your thoughts, almost like packing for a trip. Each thought or goal is like a tool that guides the discussion toward understanding and finding solutions.

When you start the conversation, being curious instead of confrontational is crucial. Ask questions that help you understand the other person's perspective, not judge it. This lets the conversation open up gradually, peeling back layers to get to the heart of the issue.

Make sure to speak from your own experiences and observations rather than making assumptions. This approach encourages openness and can turn defensive reactions into empathy and deeper connection opportunities.

Maintaining Emotional Control

Talking about sensitive topics can be like walking through a minefield of emotional triggers, where one wrong word might set off a big reaction. To handle this, it's super important to know yourself, especially what sets you off and when you're close to losing your cool. Techniques like taking deep, slow breaths can help you hit the pause button and get your emotions back in balance. You can also try visualizing how you want the conversation to go—imagine yourself staying calm and collected, which can help guide your behavior in the actual talk.

It's also key to see your emotions not as enemies but as signs. When you feel yourself getting heated, that's your cue to deal with those feelings directly. I suggest taking a break to keep the conversation productive and respectful for everyone. This way, you protect both the discussion and everyone's emotional well-being.

Creating a Safe Space for Sharing

Creating a safe space for conversation is all about creating a comfortable environment where everyone can share their feelings without worry. It starts with picking the right place—somewhere cozy and private where you won't be interrupted by everyday things. In this space, it's essential to set some basic rules like respecting each other, keeping things confidential, and letting everyone speak without cutting them off. These rules help build trust.

Showing that you're listening, whether through nods or encouraging words, makes the space feel secure. These small actions show you're engaged and care about what's being said. In a setting like this, being open and vulnerable becomes less scary and more of a way to connect, helping everyone feel supported and connected.

Follow-Up and Support

Wrapping up a tough conversation is more like hitting a milestone than reaching the end. It's a point where you can see how far you've come and what's still ahead. Follow-ups are key because they help keep the momentum from the initial talk. This could mean setting up regular check-ins to discuss how everyone's feeling or how well the agreed actions are working out. It's all about keeping up the progress towards healing and making positive changes.

Resources like books, professional help, or community support can also help. These tools give everyone what they need to handle their emotions and continue improving. Plus, ongoing support—encouraging words, kind gestures, or just being there for each other—shows that you care and are committed to each other's well-being.

This consistent support can make sensitive topics less scary, turning them into chances to grow closer and deepen your understanding and compassion as a family. This way, tough conversations become part of building a stronger, more connected family.

Family Meetings: A Tool for Democratic Household Management

Bringing together different personalities and backgrounds is key to how the household runs. One of the best ways to manage this mix is through regular family meetings, like a mini democracy. At these meetings, everyone gets a say, and decisions are made together, which helps steer the whole family's life. These gatherings are set up to be fair and include everyone, which helps build mutual respect and understanding among all family members.

Structure of Family Meetings

Starting a family meeting off right means having a clear agenda that lists all the topics you want to cover and what you hope to get done. This preparation is like getting all your ducks in a row, making sure the meeting has a clear purpose and direction. Assigning roles to each family member, like who will lead the discussion, take notes, or keep track of time, also helps make the meeting more productive and gets everyone involved.

Setting the agenda ahead of time and sharing it with everyone allows family members to suggest changes or add topics. This way, everyone has a chance to contribute to the discussion. While it's good to stick to the agenda, being flexible enough to tackle unexpected issues as they arise makes sure the meetings can adapt to whatever the family needs.

Encouraging Participation

The real power of family meetings comes from everyone getting a chance to speak up and share their views and experiences. To make sure everyone feels comfortable joining in, it's smart to use strategies that boost engagement. One good technique is to have a "speaking token"—an item you pass around, and whoever holds it gets to talk. This helps ensure even the quieter family members can speak without interruption.

Acknowledging each person's input as valuable also makes everyone feel their opinions matter, encouraging even the shy ones to open up. For younger kids, using visual aids or simple questions can help them get involved and connect their thoughts to the broader discussion.

This way, participating isn't just something family members feel they should do; it becomes a valued right that everyone actively takes part in, helping to build a family culture that's inclusive and respectful.

Resolving Issues Democratically

Solving issues in family meetings is like finding the best path forward when everyone has their ideas and solutions. It's about bringing all these viewpoints together, guided by fairness, so the final decisions reflect the group's wants and needs. Voting is a great way to ensure everyone's opinion gets counted after everyone has had a chance to discuss the issues. For critical decisions that will affect everyone's life, it's crucial to talk through compromises and negotiations, showing how much everyone values sticking together and finding solutions that make everyone reasonably happy.

This process is a mini-lesson in democracy and compromise, teaching family members valuable skills about working together and respecting different opinions. These skills are important beyond home life and affect how they handle situations in the wider world.

Celebrating Successes

Family meetings are a great time to shine a light on all the big and small wins, whether it's someone's academic success, a personal goal achieved, or something the whole family has accomplished together. Recognizing these achievements during these meetings makes them feel even more special and important. This habit helps build a culture where everyone feels appreciated and supported, strengthening the idea that the family is a team cheering for each other's successes. Celebrating these moments brings everyone joy and motivates and builds pride, adding to the family's story with tales of resilience and mutual support.

Family meetings become key to managing things democratically in blended families, where different lives and traditions unite to create a unique home life. They're more than just a way to organize; they're vital for getting everyone involved, resolving issues fairly, and celebrating wins together. This makes family meetings the heart of the home, keeping the family connected through a steady rhythm of shared experiences, respect, and joint achievements. As we continue exploring how to communicate and manage things together, these meetings shed light on navigating and cherishing the complexities and joys of living in a blended family.

THREE

Blending Parenting Styles: Crafting Harmony from Diversity

Blending different parenting styles in a family is about taking the best parts of each approach. Like pieces of fabric in a quilt, each parenting style has unique qualities. Combining these styles can complement each other and create a strong, effective parenting strategy. This doesn't just help the parents; it benefits everyone in the family, making the family unit stronger, more united, and better for everyone involved.

Understanding Each Other's Parenting Styles

Acknowledging Differences

On a typical Saturday morning, you might find a stepparent letting the kids whip up their breakfast, turning the kitchen into a hub of creative chaos with a few spills. At the same time, the biological parent might lean towards a neater, safer approach, preferring to keep things under control with some adult supervision and clear tasks. This isn't a recipe for conflict but rather a glimpse into the variety of approaches within the family. Recognizing these different styles is key to harmonious co-parenting. It's about moving from a mindset of "my way or the highway" to "our way together" and understanding that whether it's about giving independence or providing structure, both approaches are really about helping the kids grow in the best way possible.

Identifying Core Values

During a Sunday dinner, when the family sits down to discuss the week ahead, it's a great time to discuss everyone's goals and expectations. This isn't just about planning; it's also a chance to bring family values like responsibility, respect, and kindness into the conversation, especially when discussing things like homework, chores, or personal projects. These discussions help parents explain the values that guide their parenting. By focusing on these common values, the family can create a parenting approach that works with different styles and helps everyone achieve the same goals. It's not just about getting along—it's about helping the whole family thrive.

Open Dialogue

Imagine a family meeting where everyone, kids and adults, gets to talk about how things are going at home, including how parenting is handled. This open, no-judgment meeting encourages everyone to be honest and respectful. It's a place where everyone can give constructive feedback, like when a kid might want more freedom or a parent might express worries about safety. These conversations help the family work through rough spots by blending different parenting styles and finding areas where they can improve together. It's all about building a way to communicate where everyone's views are taken seriously and worked on. This helps everyone feel like they're truly part of the team regarding family decisions.

Seeking Professional Guidance

Imagine a family meeting where everyone, kids and adults, gets to talk about how things are going at home, including how parenting is handled. This open, no-judgment meeting encourages everyone to be honest and respectful. It's a place where everyone can give constructive feedback, like when a kid might want more freedom or a parent might express worries about safety. These conversations help the family work through rough spots by blending different parenting styles and finding areas where they can improve together. It's all about building a way to communicate where everyone's views are taken seriously and worked on. This helps everyone feel like they're truly part of the team regarding family decisions.

Finding Common Ground: Creating Unified Parenting Strategies

Compromise and adaptation are crucial when developing a parenting strategy in a blended family. Here, compromising doesn't mean giving up what you stand for. It's more about a balanced give-and-take, where everyone's viewpoints merge into a solid, agreed-upon approach. This balancing act needs a good handle on negotiation, ensuring that when one person gives a little, the other responds with kindness, leading to a plan everyone can get behind. As things in family life keep changing, adaptation becomes necessary, allowing family strategies to evolve and meet new needs and challenges.

It's also key to set clear, consistent guidelines to keep everyone on the same page. Creating these rules takes careful thought to ensure they reflect what the family stands for together. Everyone, adults and kids alike, should have a say in this process, making the rules a reliable standard for behavior and decisions that help avoid confusion and conflict, giving a sense of stability and teamwork.

Family meetings play a huge role here. They're a regular space where the family can come together to talk over and tweak their strategies. This ongoing conversation keeps the parenting approach practical and relevant, adjusting to individual and family needs. It's a way to emphasize that handling family life is a team effort.

Role modeling is another big piece. How parents and stepparents act day-to-day teaches kids a lot. Adults set a strong example by showing unity, respect, and cooperation. This isn't just about steering clear of arguments; it's actively showing how to handle problems, show empathy, and understand others. Kids pick up on these behaviors, learning important values and how to interact with others.

In trying to blend different parenting styles into one effective strategy, families embark on a journey full of negotiation, creativity, and commitment to shared goals. Through compromise, setting clear rules, holding regular family meetings, and leading by example, blended families work through their unique challenges, building a strong, resilient approach to parenting. This way, they manage and celebrate their diversity, creating a path filled with understanding, respect, and unity. This journey enhances not just the blending of styles but the thriving of the whole family.

Discipline in Blended Families: A Balanced Approach

Consistent Discipline

Setting a discipline strategy in a blended family is like solving a puzzle. You're trying to merge everyone's beliefs, backgrounds, and expectations into a plan that fits everyone in the household. The aim is to ensure that the rules and their application remain consistent no matter who's in charge. This helps ensure everyone is clear and on board, which maintains stability.

The process usually starts with in-depth discussions where each adult shares their thoughts on discipline. Building from these conversations, you can put together a family handbook. This handbook is more than just a list of rules; it's a collaboratively created guide that sets out the expected behaviors and the consequences for not sticking to them. And it's flexible—it evolves as the family does, ensuring it stays relevant and reflects the family's ongoing needs while maintaining core values.

Understanding Emotional Underpinnings

Mixed emotions often fuel Kids' behavior, especially in a blended family. Sometimes, they might act out or become withdrawn, and it's not just about being difficult—they could be feeling uncertain about their new family situation or missing how things used to be. For parents and stepparents, it's crucial to dig deeper and figure out what's going on behind those actions.

To get to the heart of it, you must observe, listen well, and ask open-ended questions that get them talking more than just "yes" or "no." This gives them space to open up about their feelings and helps them understand the more significant reasons behind their behavior.

With this deeper insight, they manage discipline, shifting from just trying to correct unwanted behavior to really connecting with your child. It's about helping them work through their emotions and guiding them toward better behavior, not just for the sake of rules but for their emotional growth and better understanding of their feelings.

Stepparent Involvement

Discipline in a blended family can put stepparents in a tough spot. They need to figure out how to effectively step in while still respecting the role of the biological parents. Making this work requires plenty of discussion and clear agreements between all the parents to make sure everyone understands the stepparent's role in discipline.

When it's time for a stepparent to take charge of disciplining, it's crucial that what they do aligns with the agreed-upon family discipline plan. This ensures their actions aren't surprising but are consistent with what the family expects. The key here is to present a united front, showing the kids that all the adults, biological or not, are on the same page with discipline. This unity is essential for creating a stable and secure environment for the kids.

Positive Reinforcement

Positive reinforcement is a way to manage discipline. This approach focuses on encouraging good behavior by acknowledging and rewarding it rather than just focusing on punishing the bad. It creates an environment where kids are motivated to behave well because they look forward to positive feedback, not because they're scared of consequences.

You could set up a system where good behaviors that align with your family's values are rewarded, or it might be as simple as giving a shout-out when someone does something great. This positive feedback makes kids feel recognized and appreciated, encouraging them to continue behaving well. The idea is that people, including kids, naturally gravitate toward actions that bring them positive outcomes, linking good behavior with feelings of happiness and fulfillment.

Positive reinforcement does more than just manage behavior—it reflects the family's dedication to supporting and encouraging each other's growth and success. It helps guide kids to follow the rules and understand and internalize the values those rules represent.

Celebrating Individuality While Ensuring Consistency

Balancing everyone's unique personalities with the house rules is key in a blended family. Pay attention to what each child needs and ensure the family's values don't diminish their individuality. This approach sees the differences between family members as strengths that enhance the family experience.

A big challenge in blended families is ensuring all the kids feel equally cared for, avoiding any feelings of favoritism or neglect. One way to handle this is by spending quality time with each child, doing things that match their interests and where they are in life. Whether reading a book together at bedtime or going on a hike, these moments send a clear message: you matter, and you're an essential part of this family.

Another key part is involving everyone in decisions. Whether choosing what to have for dinner or planning a vacation, listening to and considering everyone's opinion helps build a strong sense of belonging and respect. This includes talking about the tougher stuff that affects how everyone feels and relates to each other, reinforcing the bonds within the family.

As kids grow, their needs and independence change, so the family's approach might need some tweaking to stay in tune with these changes. This could mean updating the rules to give older kids more freedom or changing how you communicate with teens. Staying flexible shows a commitment to supporting each child as they grow, ensuring that family guidelines remain helpful and relevant.

This ongoing process of balancing individual needs with family consistency requires constant re-evaluation and adaptation. Blended families can create a supportive environment that values individuality and unity by focusing on what each family member needs, ensuring everyone's voice is heard, and adjusting as kids grow. This approach keeps the family strong and celebrates its diversity, making the family life richer and more connected.

Handling Backlash: When Kids Challenge Unified Fronts

Navigating Resistance

In a blended family, it's common for kids and teens to resist parenting decisions. Often, this resistance is their way of processing all the new changes. They might be feeling scared, confused, or just craving more independence. Understanding why they're resisting is like putting together a puzzle—each act of defiance helps you piece together their feelings.

A good approach is to talk it out calmly. Ask them questions that show you're truly interested in their point of view, and try to do this when everyone's emotions are more settled. This patient and thoughtful way of handling things can turn tough moments into chances for genuine connection. By listening to what's on their mind, you can figure out how to give them more freedom while maintaining the family's overall rules and values.

Maintaining Open Communication

It's important to keep everyone talking openly when facing resistance and backlash in a blended family. The goal is to have a continuous, honest conversation that helps everyone stay connected. This kind of talk should be free from judgment and scolding, creating a safe space where kids can express their concerns, frustrations, and hopes while feeling heard and valued. It's about listening to truly understand them, not just waiting for your turn to respond, and approaching each conversation with empathy.

Trust builds in this open environment, where people can discuss their thoughts and feelings without fear. This strengthens the kids' sense of security and belonging in the family. Keeping up this level of openness requires a lot of effort. You have to be proactive about tackling issues as they arise and dedicated to ensuring the home feels welcoming, where everyone, regardless of age, feels comfortable speaking their mind and believing they'll be understood.

Unified Response

How parents handle challenges in a blended family sets the tone for the whole household. Having a united front, where all the parents and stepparents are on the same page about managing parenting decisions, creates a solid and dependable structure for kids to lean on. This unity comes from forming a strong team where everyone respects each other and aims for the same goals, managing disagreements privately, and always presenting a supportive front to the kids.

Although it might seem simple, achieving this takes a lot of teamwork and honest communication among the adults. It involves having regular discussions to ensure everyone agrees on discipline, house rules, and how to react to the kids' behaviors. The true strength of this unified approach goes beyond just consistency; it also shows the kids that, no matter how complex their family situation might be, they are in a safe and secure place where every decision is made with their best interests at heart. This helps them feel stable and safe, even when the outside world seems chaotic.

Support and Reassurance

In a blended family, as everything changes, kids and teens need continuous support and reassurance to adjust to the new family setup and what's expected. This support is more than just being there for them when they're upset; it's about making sure they feel like a true part of the family. This comes through in the quiet moments when you comfort them after a disagreement, remind them daily that they're loved, and patiently explain why things are changing at home.

Supporting them this way means paying attention to their feelings, guessing what they might need before they ask, and always responding with encouragement and recognition. It's about being present, offering a steady hand to hold, and reassuring words that help them feel secure and welcomed in their new family environment. This kind of steady and unconditional support is crucial because it builds their resilience, giving them the confidence to tackle the world, knowing they are valued, loved, and supported no matter what.

Stepparenting: Roles, Boundaries, and Building Relationships

In a blended family, as everything changes, kids and teens need continuous support and reassurance to adjust to the new family setup and what's expected. This support is more than just being there for them when they're upset; it's about making sure they feel like a true part of the family. This comes through in the quiet moments when you comfort them after a disagreement, remind them daily that they're loved, and patiently explain why things are changing at home.

Supporting them this way means paying attention to their feelings, guessing what they might need before they ask, and always responding with encouragement and recognition. It's about being present, offering a steady hand to hold, and reassuring words that help them feel secure and welcomed in their new family environment. This kind of steady and unconditional support is crucial because it builds their resilience, giving them the confidence to tackle the world, knowing they are valued, loved, and supported no matter what.

FOUR

Managing Relationships with Ex-Partners and Extended Family

Dealing with ex-partners and extended family can get complicated in blended family life. Co-parenting with an ex involves handling old emotions and current responsibilities. Every conversation and decision about boundaries must be handled carefully, with the main goal always being to support the kids' well-being.

Co-Parenting with Ex-Partners: Keeping Kids First

Prioritizing Children's Well-Being

In co-parenting, "children come first" guides all the decisions and interactions. It means that the kids' needs and well-being should always take priority over any leftover hard feelings or disagreements between ex-partners. For example, consider attending parent-teacher conferences or school plays where you must be around your ex. In these situations, it's crucial to put aside personal discomfort and focus on what matters—like the pride or concern you see in your child's eyes. This shows how important it is to present a united front as parents to support your child's education and emotional well-being.

Effective Communication

Successful co-parenting hinges on strong, respectful communication. It's all about getting past any old issues to ensure you can easily share important things like schedules, kids' achievements, and concerns. Co-parenting apps are super helpful for this. They simplify communication and help avoid misunderstandings. These apps act like a neutral space where you can exchange information—from doctor's appointments to weekend plans—without dealing with the stress of direct conversations. This helps keep the focus on organizing things smoothly for the benefit of the kids.

Setting Boundaries

Setting clear boundaries is key in managing where ex-partners have influence and how involved they can be. These boundaries help protect the new blended family's space while ensuring kids can easily connect with both parents. For example, setting specific times for phone calls or visits helps prevent one household's routines from disrupting the other's, keeping things harmonious and respectful. These boundaries, which should be worked out considering the kids' schedules and needs, ensure their lives transition smoothly between the two homes, keeping them shielded from any potential conflict between their parents.

Co-Parenting Agreements

Solid co-parenting relationships often start with making some formal or informal agreements. These can be drawn up with a lawyer or written down at home. Either way, they lay out who is responsible for what set expectations and explain how to handle disagreements, acting as a roadmap for how to work together. These agreements cover everything from who pays for what to who gets the kids during holidays, making the co-parenting relationship more structured and predictable. For kids navigating life between two homes, these agreements are like a promise that they'll always have love, attention, and support from both parents, no matter what's going on with them.

In the big picture of co-parenting, where past and present often overlap, focusing on the kids' well-being, keeping communication clear, setting boundaries, and writing down co-parenting plans helps everyone move forward in a way that puts the kids first. When carried out with thoughtfulness and respect, these approaches help ensure that despite the challenges of a blended family setup, the children's growing experience is filled with love, stability, and strong support from all their parents.

Visual Element: Co-Parenting Communication Plan Template

A co-parenting communication plan template can help establish effective ways to talk and coordinate between co-parents. This tool lays out important stuff like schedules, emergency contacts, and who handles what financially. It gives you a clear format to write agreements and keep communication straightforward. The template is great for kicking off discussions, ensuring ex-partners think about everything they need to manage together and helping them spot and sort out possible issues before they become real problems.

Navigating Extended Family Dynamics in Blended Families

In a blended family, connections include many extended family members. These relationships are often complex and full of history, and it takes a careful approach to keep everything harmonious and ensure everyone feels included in this new family setup.

Inclusive Celebrations

Organizing family events and celebrations in a blended family is about finding the right balance. You want to respect everyone's traditions while creating a welcoming atmosphere that includes the whole family. Planning these events means choosing dates, places, and activities that reflect all family members' backgrounds and tastes. For example, when setting up a holiday party, you could mix food, music, and decorations from each family's cultural traditions. This way, everyone's heritage gets a nod, making the celebration richer and showing the unity and respect at the heart of the new family setup. Moments like these help break down barriers and strengthen family ties, celebrating the diverse heritage that each person brings to the table.

Addressing Biases

Dealing with biases and prejudices from extended family members requires a patient and thoughtful approach. It's all about opening up conversations and tackling these issues with a mix of understanding and firmness. This means starting discussions that show how these biases affect everyone in the family. You need to be ready to listen and get to the heart of where these attitudes are coming from while also standing your ground by sharing personal stories and pointing out the strengths and unity of your blended family. This isn't easy and can be emotionally taxing, but it's necessary to pave the way for meaningful changes. These conversations can gradually change old perceptions and create a more welcoming and accepting family atmosphere. Over time, these talks plant the seeds of understanding and respect, breaking down prejudices and helping everyone appreciate the unique richness of your blended family.

Role of Grandparents

Grandparents have a special place in the family, often holding onto traditions and connecting different generations. In a blended family, they can play a supportive role, offering everything from help with school and hobbies to sharing their life experiences for emotional support. However, ensuring grandparents fit smoothly into the family mix requires setting clear boundaries and expectations. This way, their involvement enhances rather than clashes with the parenting style and values the parents are trying to establish.

Having open and honest conversations about these boundaries allows for a cooperative relationship where grandparents feel appreciated and included, yet the parents' roles and rules are still respected. When this balance is struck, grandparents aren't just visitors; they're valuable allies who contribute to the family's overall harmony and help support the growth and happiness of the grandchildren. This teamwork adds to the family's rich, intergenerational dynamic.

Maintaining Relationships

Keeping up relationships with extended family in a blended family requires continuous communication, flexibility, and understanding. It's about recognizing that each relationship, whether with aunts, uncles, or cousins, has its history and importance and needs to be nurtured. Balancing your blended family's immediate needs and routines with staying connected to your wider family network can be tricky.

You can maintain this balance by scheduling regular visits or video calls, including extended family in significant events and celebrations, and keeping an open line of communication about the changes and dynamics in your blended family. These efforts help keep the family fabric strong and vibrant, weaving each relationship into the larger story of your family's life. By managing these connections carefully, blended families can maintain a supportive network that bridges generations and backgrounds, adding depth and strength to everyone's lives.

Holidays and Special Occasions: Planning for Success

Advance Planning

Planning holidays and special events in a blended family takes a lot of careful thought and organization, considering everyone's unique traditions and schedules. It's like mapping out a detailed journey where you must start talking and planning early to ensure everyone's voices are heard and their traditions are included in the celebrations. Imagine a calendar with events color-coded by each part of the family's heritage—a clear visual that helps prevent scheduling clashes and ensures everyone's customs are respected.

Strategic planning helps avoid stress and turns the process into a unifying activity. It's not just about getting through these events; it's about looking forward to the joy they bring and experiencing them together as a family.

Creating New Traditions

Starting new traditions in a blended family is a great way to build a shared identity, mixing everyone's past customs with new ideas to create unique celebrations. Think about creating a special holiday for your family, celebrating the day you all came together. You could create rituals and activities everyone helps design, showing how far you've come as a team. These new traditions, drawn from everyone's different backgrounds, become key moments that help write your family's shared story. They fill your calendar with meaningful dates special to your family, strengthening everyone's sense of belonging and connection.

Involving Children

Getting kids involved in planning and running holiday events and special occasions is key to a successful celebration in a blended family. This isn't just about giving everyone a say; it's an important way for kids to share what they're excited about or even worried about when it comes to blending family traditions. They might pick out dishes that reflect their cultural backgrounds or choose decorations that match their style. Letting them participate shows you value their input and helps you understand how they see themselves fitting into the family. Plus, working together teaches them how to compromise and the joy of creating something new from their diverse backgrounds, which can make them proud of their family's unique traditions.

Navigating Emotional Challenges

Holidays and special occasions in a blended family can feel like a rollercoaster of emotions, with moments of happiness mixing with sadness. This mix reflects the blend of memories, the loss of old traditions, and the start of new connections. Handling these feelings well requires a thoughtful and caring approach, recognizing that feeling sad about what's gone or anxious about new changes is okay. One way to deal with these feelings is by having open talks where everyone's emotions are accepted without judgment, setting aside private time for individuals to celebrate in their way, and reassuring everyone that it's normal to have mixed feelings.

Support can come from one-on-one chats, family therapy, or just the knowledge that the family supports each other no matter what. These efforts help build an environment where emotional challenges are met with understanding and compassion, turning potential conflicts into chances to strengthen family ties.

As you navigate life in a blended family, holidays and special events offer great opportunities to celebrate together, honor different backgrounds, and create new memories. Through careful planning, starting new traditions, involving the kids, and sensitively handling emotional ups and downs, these celebrations can become key moments of togetherness and love. They add depth to the family's ongoing story, strengthening the connections within the family and affirming its unique character and unity amid its complexity.

Setting Boundaries with Ex-Partners and Extended Family

In a blended family, managing relationships with ex-partners and extended family members is like walking a tightrope—it requires careful and thoughtful handling. Just like adjusting settings on delicate machinery, maintaining healthy boundaries is crucial. These boundaries need clear communication, firm but kind enforcement, support from current family members, and the flexibility to adjust as the family's needs change. This balancing act helps keep everything running smoothly and ensures everyone knows where they stand, essential for keeping peace and respect in the family.

Clear Communication

Navigating blended family life means having a communication strategy that's smart, thoughtful, and aims to solve problems rather than create them. Setting boundaries with ex-partners and extended family starts with clear and open conversations. It's about language that brings people together, not pushes them apart. This kind of talk is like mapping out where everyone stands, ensuring the lines drawn help everyone understand each other better and balancing individual needs with what's best for the group. When talking about things like visitation, holidays, or who does what, the goal is to reach a place where everyone gets it and respects it, creating a space where the kids' well-being is the top priority everyone agrees on.

Enforcing Boundaries

Once you set boundaries in a blended family, sticking to them can test everyone's resolve, just like navigating a tricky situation. Keeping these boundaries strong against any pushback or conflict means consistently following the rules you've all agreed on and fairly applying consequences if those rules are broken. This should be done firmly but kindly—think flexible strength rather than harsh rigidity.

When these boundaries are challenged, it's helpful to remind everyone why they were set in the first place. Reaffirming the reasons can help everyone remember that these rules were made considering the family's best interests. By staying firm but understanding, the family can maintain its structure and harmony, ensuring those boundaries keep the peace and support everyone's well-being.

Supporting Each Other

In a blended family, setting and keeping boundaries works best when everyone supports each other. This teamwork is like the roots of a tree, keeping it stable through any storm. When one family member struggles to enforce a boundary, whether with an ex-partner or another relative, everyone else offers emotional backing and practical help. This united approach is crucial in protecting the family from outside stress, ensuring everyone sticks together and respects the family's rules. By standing firm together, the family strengthens its ties and clarifies to everyone else that they're serious about their boundaries and values.

Adjusting as Needed

In a blended family, boundaries need to be as adaptable as life itself, changing with the evolving needs and situations of the family. This flexibility doesn't mean indecisiveness; it shows a mature understanding that the family's needs are always shifting and a commitment to proactively addressing these changes. Whether it's because the kids are growing up, living situations are changing, or relationships with ex-partners and extended family are evolving, it's crucial to revisit and adjust boundaries accordingly. Talking these changes through and making thoughtful adjustments ensures that these boundaries support the family's growth and harmony.

In managing blended family dynamics, it's vital to carefully set, enforce, support, and adapt boundaries with ex-partners and extended family. By communicating, enforcing boundaries firmly, backing each other up, and staying open to necessary changes, the family can handle its complex relationships with unity and grace. These efforts, always aimed at the family's best interests, help maintain a strong, vibrant family dynamic that can handle the ups and downs unique to blended family life.

The Role of the Ex-Partner in Your Blended Family

Defining the Role

When putting together a blended family, dealing with ex-partners can be tricky. It is important to find the right balance between respecting the ex-partner's relationship with their kids and keeping the new family unit functioning independently. This balance starts with an open conversation among all the adults involved, aiming to understand clearly what role the ex-partner will play. This might involve setting specific areas where the ex-partner's input is helpful and appreciated, like matters directly affecting the kids' welfare or education while ensuring other decisions stay within the new family unit.

Mapping out these boundaries carefully ensures that while the ex-partner remains an important part of the children's lives, they don't step over into managing the new family's internal dynamics. This approach requires a lot of sensitivity and respect from everyone to create a supportive environment that benefits the kids' growth and happiness.

Communication Guidelines

Setting up clear and practical communication guidelines is essential for handling the role of an ex-partner in a blended family. These guidelines help keep conversations respectful and focused on the kids' needs, steering clear of any old conflicts. It's helpful to agree on how and how often you'll update each other, whether through regular meetings, emails, or a digital co-parenting platform. Having a structured way to communicate can prevent misunderstandings and encourage a teamwork approach centered on what's best for the kids. If tensions start to flare, sticking to these agreed-upon guidelines can help keep discussions productive and focused, reducing the chance of conflict and ensuring the conversations benefit the kids.

Involvement in Decisions

In blended families, making decisions can get pretty complex because you're bringing together a bunch of different viewpoints, each with its merit. Including ex-partners in decisions that affect the kids shows a commitment to comprehensive care and consideration. However, it's important to manage how this input fits in, balancing it with the blended family's need to make decisions independently. For big issues like education, health, or significant life changes, it's good to have a space where everyone can discuss things openly, allowing ex-partners to share their thoughts in a way that respects their relationship with the kids. At the same time, it's crucial to be clear about who has the final say, ensuring that the primary caregivers make the decisions. This approach creates a cooperative environment where the ex-partner's input is valued but doesn't interfere with the new family's structure.

Managing Expectations

Managing expectations is key to having a good relationship with an ex-partner in a blended family setting. This means setting clear boundaries about how involved the ex-partner should be and keeping emotions in check during interactions. Recognizing that everyone is adjusting to the new family setup can ease resentment or feeling left out. Having regular check-ins where adults can discuss and adjust their expectations can stop misunderstandings or frustrations from growing. It's also important to create a space where everyone feels safe to express concerns or disappointment and knows they'll be met with empathy. This open communication helps solve problems before they get bigger.

Navigating the ex-partner's role requires balancing their involvement with maintaining the family's independence. By clearly defining this role and establishing effective communication, blended families can build a supportive environment that respects all relationships. Including the ex-partner thoughtfully in decisions that affect the kids and carefully managing everyone's expectations helps maintain a relationship based on mutual respect and a shared focus on the kids' happiness. This approach fosters a cooperative family life and understanding and is deeply committed to creating a nurturing and harmonious atmosphere.

Creating a Support System Within and Outside the Family

Strong support inside and outside the home is crucial in a blended family. Building trust and mutual support can help the family face its unique challenges. This might look like regular family dinners, creating shared rituals, or keeping communication open, ensuring everyone feels connected and committed to each other's well-being. These aren't just regular meetings; they're key times when the family can bond and tackle any issues, strengthening their connections.

Beyond the home, it helps to reach out for extra support. This might involve joining support groups, seeing counselors, or connecting with online communities that understand what blended families go through. These resources are great for picking up tips and feeling less alone, as they reflect the shared experiences of others in similar situations.

Engaging with friends and the wider community is another great layer of support. Friends, neighbors, and community members can offer new perspectives on family life, practical help, and a sense of belonging. Whether through community events, casual meetups, or local activities, these connections enrich the family's life and help it feel more integrated into the wider world.

The ongoing effort to build and maintain relationships within and outside the family is at the core of all this. This requires patience, openness, and a commitment to growing together. The family learns that its strength comes as much from internal unity as from its connections with the wider world, investing in these relationships as a fundamental part of its identity and resilience.

Blended families can create a robust support network by supporting each other within the family and reaching out for external guidance and community connection. This network helps them handle daily challenges and enriches their lives, making the family journey smoother and more fulfilling. This chapter highlights how important a strong support system is, both inside the home and beyond, as families navigate the complexities of blended life together, growing stronger and more connected.

FIVE

Financial Harmony in Blended Families

In a blended family home full of laughter and warmth, finances are often an unspoken but important issue. Money impacts everything, from security to opportunities and sometimes even creates tension. Addressing this topic in blended families, where everyone might have different financial backgrounds, is crucial for maintaining peace and understanding.

Combining Finances: A Step-by-Step Guide

Assessing Financial Situations

Before starting real financial planning in a blended family, you need a complete understanding of everyone's financial situation. This means looking deeper than just scanning through bank statements—it's like putting together a puzzle where you need to fit together pieces like income, debts, obligations, and assets. To be honest, from the start, as you sit in the living room or around the kitchen table with your financial documents and laptops open, discuss and reveal the numbers that will guide your family's financial plans. While this initial step might seem overwhelming, it's essential for breaking down barriers and creating a shared understanding of your financial reality, helping everyone move forward together with a clear view.

Joint Versus Separate Accounts

Deciding between joint and separate accounts is a big choice for blended families, and both options have pros and cons. All the money goes into one pot with joint accounts, making handling household expenses easier. Still, it also means you need a lot of trust and open communication between everyone. Separate accounts keep individual spending separate, which can reduce arguments over personal purchases but might make it harder to manage shared bills. Many blended families go for a mix of both—a joint account for household costs and separate accounts for personal spending. This combo allows you to manage home expenses together while having your own money for personal needs.

Creating a Unified Budget

Putting together a budget for a blended family is like getting everyone's finances to play nicely together. It starts with setting common goals—saving for a family trip, covering everyday household costs, or putting money away for future education. Everyone pitches in, bringing their incomes, expenses, savings, and debts to craft a budget that fits the family's needs and limits. You can think of spreadsheets as your roadmap here, where every category and allocation is laid out, ready to be tweaked as things change. This budget isn't set in stone; regular check-ups and tweaks are needed to stay useful. It guides the family's financial choices, ensuring everything lines up to keep the family on track financially.

Legal and Financial Advice

Trying to blend a family's finances without professional help is like navigating without a map. Lawyers and financial advisors are like your guides—they can provide specialized advice tailored to your family's unique needs. Whether it's figuring out how to combine assets or handling things like child support and alimony, these experts can help clear up any confusion and show you options you might not have considered on your own. Their advice ensures that everything from how your accounts are set up to planning your estate is done right, keeping you in line with the law and financial best practices. Getting their help early on can steady your family's financial ship, helping you manage the complex finances of a blended family with more confidence.

Vision Element: Budget Planning Worksheet

A budget planning worksheet is necessary when creating a blended family budget. This worksheet is designed to handle the unique financial details of blended families, with sections for different income sources, fixed and variable expenses, savings targets, and debts. It comes with prompts that help you think through every financial detail, from daily spending to long-term goals. Not only does it help in planning, but it also gets conversations started—conversations that might otherwise be missed. You can download it, update it regularly, and use it as a key part of your family's financial strategy, making setting a budget more doable and something you can work on together.

These steps—getting a clear picture of everyone's finances, deciding between joint and separate accounts, using a worksheet to make a unified budget, and getting advice from professionals—act like signposts as you handle the financial challenges of a blended family life. They help navigate the tricky parts of merging finances, turning potential stress points into chances for greater unity and understanding. By dealing with finances openly, honestly, and cooperatively, blended families can create a strong financial foundation that supports a stable and thriving family life.

Child Support and Alimony: Navigating the Legal Landscape

Understanding Legal Obligations

In blended families, dealing with financial obligations like child support and alimony can get pretty complicated because the rules change depending on where you live. Understanding these obligations isn't just about knowing the legal contracts but also about grasping how deeply these responsibilities are connected to the heart of family life. It starts with getting a handle on the various laws that dictate how much, how long, and under what conditions these payments are made, which can differ greatly from one place to another.

For families trying to figure this out, talking to a legal professional who's up to speed on the local laws is crucial. They can help you make sense of the complex legal details and ensure that whatever steps you take are in the best interest of the family's well-being.

Impact on Family Finances

Child support and alimony payments are significant factors in a family's finances, shaping everything from how you handle daily expenses to how you plan for the future. These payments are more than just numbers; they play a big role in how the family manages money. To effectively integrate these payments into your financial planning, being open and working together is crucial. This means figuring out the exact amounts and ensuring they fit into the family's overall budget, including everyday costs, saving for goals, and paying off debts. Handling it this way helps keep the family's finances stable, allowing you to manage your financial responsibilities without losing track of longer-term financial health and growth.

Modifications and Adjustments

As life changes, so does a family's financial situation, which can lead to a need to update child support and alimony orders. This could be due to anything from a change in income or job status to shifts in the kids' needs or the financial situation of the person receiving the payments. Adjusting these orders is a bit like changing sails on a boat to match the wind—you need to do it to keep things balanced and on course. The process for making these changes is pretty strict and usually requires showing that there's been a big change in circumstances. For families thinking about this, having a lawyer to guide you is helpful. They can explain what needs to be proven, what documents you'll need, and how to proceed. Legal advice and keeping everyone in the loop helps ensure the adjustment process is fair and considers everyone's needs, keeping the family's financial situation stable as things change.

Communication with Ex-Partners

Effectively managing child support and alimony depends on how well you communicate with your ex-partner. It's all about being clear and considerate in your conversations, which can help prevent misunderstandings and conflicts. Good communication goes beyond just sharing numbers; it involves openly discussing concerns, updating each other on financial changes, and being willing to discuss adjustments as needed. Setting up regular times to check in and speak respectfully without dragging in old emotional baggage can make a big difference. If talking directly is too difficult, a mediator or legal help can be a good alternative. This way, you can still have productive discussions about finances without straining your co-parenting relationship. By keeping these lines of communication open, families can handle child support and alimony responsibly, ensuring everyone's financial needs are met and contributing to the overall financial stability of the family.

Saving for the Future: Education, Emergencies and Retirement

Managing money in a blended family is super important, especially regarding saving. It's not just about putting money aside but planning how to use that savings to help the family reach its goals and secure its future. One of the biggest challenges is figuring out how to balance saving for immediate needs, long-term dreams, and those unexpected emergencies that pop up. It's like trying to steer a ship through tricky waters, where you must keep an eye on everything to ensure you're heading in the right direction.

Prioritizing Savings Goals

Saving money in a blended family starts with a clear look at what you aim for—setting money aside for the kids' education, building an emergency fund, and saving for retirement. You need a plan that spreads your resources across these goals so nothing gets left out. It's like having a team meeting to map out a journey, considering which goals need immediate attention and which are more about the long haul. This isn't just a one-time chat; it's an ongoing conversation that adapts as your family's needs and dreams grow and change, ensuring your money always aligns with your life's current and future needs.

Strategies for Saving

Once the family's savings goals are set, the next step is figuring out how to get there—think of it as setting the sails to catch the wind. Setting up automated transfers is a great start. This moves a set amount of money straight into savings before it can be spent. Using tax-advantaged accounts like 529 plans for education or IRAs for retirement can help, too, as these accounts allow your savings to grow without taking a hit from taxes. If you have access to employer-sponsored retirement plans or savings programs that match your contributions, those are like having an extra push that helps your savings grow faster. Combining all these strategies gives you a solid plan to help you meet your savings goals more efficiently and effectively.

Involving Children in Saving Plans

Bringing kids into the family financial planning process is a crucial step. It's more than just teaching them about money; it's about getting involved in managing their financial future. When you talk about saving for college, it's a chance for them to understand the value of money and what it means to plan and sacrifice to reach their goals. Giving them their savings accounts turns into a real-life lesson where they can see how interest and growth work over time, making these ideas more real and understandable. This kind of hands-on experience teaches them how money works and gives them a sense of responsibility and ownership over their finances. It prepares them with the skills to handle money wisely as adults.

Balancing Competing Needs

Managing finances in a blended family involves juggling various needs, like education, emergency funds, and retirement savings. It's about balancing spending for today with saving for the future. Open discussions about priorities and possible sacrifices are crucial. This helps the family create a balanced savings plan that respects everyone's needs and works together to build a financial plan that reflects the family's goals and strengths.

Blended families must gather when saving for big things like education, emergencies, and retirement. It's about setting priorities, figuring out how to save effectively, getting kids involved in the finances, and ensuring everyone's needs get a fair hearing. This kind of teamwork sets the family on a path to financial stability and satisfaction. By working through these challenges together, the family doesn't just shore up its financial future—it also strengthens the personal ties that hold it together, stepping forward with confidence and a clear plan to achieve their shared dreams.

Daily Financial Management in a Blended Family

Managing daily finances in a blended family is a crucial, sometimes overlooked, part of family life. It's all about keeping track of the money coming in and going out, and you need to stay sharp to keep everything running smoothly. Having a daily spending plan is key. It's more than just a list of what you spend; it's a dynamic tool that reflects what the family values and aims for. This plan helps everyone stay on track with their financial goals, ensuring the family's money matters stay peaceful and organized.

Creating a Daily Spending Plan

Creating a daily spending plan is more than dividing up your money. It's a chance to think about your spending, plan for what's coming, and make trade-offs. This plan digs into the nitty-gritty of your regular spending, helping you see where your money's going and whether it's supporting your bigger financial goals. Every time you log an expense, it's a moment to decide: Do you go for the quick satisfaction or put that bit extra towards your long-term plans?

To make this easier, families might set aside specific amounts for everyday expenses, using physical envelopes or digital tools to keep things organized. This method makes your financial goals concrete, turning abstract planning into something you manage daily.

Managing Expenses

Managing a family's finances means keeping a close eye on expenses and being smart about spending. This involves looking at all your regular costs—everything from the small stuff to the big bills—and finding ways to save money without cutting back on living well. You could buy in bulk for everyday items, reduce energy use, or choose memorable experiences over buying things.

Another big part of managing money is keeping a tight leash on the fun spending, which can easily get out of hand. Setting up allowances is a great way to handle this. It gives everyone a bit of independence but keeps spending within set limits. This helps teach responsible spending habits and lets family members treat themselves without going overboard.

Tracking and Review

Sticking to a daily spending plan depends on keeping close tabs on your spending and checking in regularly to see how you're doing. It's like navigating by the stars—you've got to keep an eye on your course, spot when you're off track, and figure out why. This is all about being open and accountable. Every expense gets logged and checked out, not to point fingers, but to see what's happening with your money and to adjust habits as needed.

Regular family meetings to discuss finances are a great way to do this. These aren't just boring sit-downs; they're a chance for everyone to talk about money openly, learn from what's happening, and ensure everyone's on the same page. This way, managing money becomes a team effort that keeps you in line with your financial goals, boosts everyone's understanding of money and pulls the family together.

Financial Software and Tools

Today, there's a ton of financial software and tools out there that can help families handle their money better. These digital helpers, from budgeting apps to expense trackers, do more than save time. They give you insights and real-time data on how you're spending and where you can improve. Picking the right tool means thinking about what your family needs explicitly, like how secure it is, how easy it is to use, and whether it syncs up with your banks. Once you've chosen, these tools can take over things like paying bills automatically, sorting your spending into categories, and alerting you if you're about to go over budget. When you make these tools part of your everyday money management, they can turn a chore into a chance to get on top of your finances, using tech to make everything smoother, inform your choices, and help everyone in the family become more mindful about money.

In managing their finances daily, blended families balance today's needs with tomorrow's goals. They create a financially aware environment by carefully planning daily spending, monitoring expenses, regularly checking how they're doing against their budget, and using tech tools wisely. This approach isn't just about meeting goals; it's about building strong family ties as everyone works together openly and strategically to create a secure and prosperous future.

Financial Fairness: Ensuring No Child is Left Behind

In a blended family, treating everyone fairly is a big deal—it echoes through every decision made and affects everyone. This approach to fairness in managing money is not just about being equal; it's also about being fair and inclusive, no matter if someone is a step or biological family member.

However, trying to keep things fair financially can take time and effort. Differences in resources and needs can make it tough to keep everyone feeling treated equally. You need to be creative, empathetic, and forward-thinking to handle this. You start by recognizing where there might be gaps or imbalances and then work hard to lessen their impact. This might mean setting up individual savings plans for each kid's education or fairly splitting money for activities, making sure each child feels supported and valued.

Openness and honesty are crucial when talking about money. These conversations might be tough, but they're key to understanding and trust. Being transparent—keeping no secrets about the family's finances—helps clear up doubts or worries and ensures everyone is on the same page, making decisions together.

Being flexible with your financial plans is also vital because life changes. Being ready to adjust when needed, whether because of a surprise expense or a new opportunity, helps the family stick together and react as one unit. It keeps your approach to fairness active and relevant, adapting as the family's needs change.

By focusing on fairness, a blended family does more than just manage money well. They build strong relationships based on respect and mutual support. The family creates a supportive atmosphere by treating all kids equally, openly discussing finances, adapting to changes, and balancing everyone's needs. This commitment to fairness weaves a strong bond within the family, helping everyone feel included and cared for now and in the future.

Money Conversations: Engaging the Whole Family

Talking about money is a big deal in a blended family. Regular family financial meetings aren't just routine sit-downs; they're crucial for everyone to get on the same page about budget goals and understand money matters together. These meetings clear the confusing world of finances and connect it to real family plans and dreams, helping everyone, no matter how young, to feel involved and responsible for the family's financial health.

Teaching kids and teens about money is key in these discussions. It's more than just giving them facts; it's about bringing them into the decision-making circle, a place usually just for adults. Learning about saving and spending can be fun for the little ones, like through games or small paid chores that teach them the basics. On the brink of independence, teenagers dive into more complex stuff like budgeting, how saving works over time, and the real cost of using credit, preparing them to handle their money wisely.

Setting financial goals together is another way to strengthen this team effort. It's like mapping out a journey to places the family wants to explore, from next year's vacation to college savings. Everyone, from kids to adults, gets a say, making the process a team effort where everyone supports each other's financial dreams and works through setbacks together.

Of course, not everyone will always agree, and financial disagreements can pop up. Handling these moments well is crucial to keeping family ties strong. Listening to each other, trying to understand different points of view, and finding compromises help keep small disagreements from turning into big fights. Bringing in a neutral third party like a financial advisor can help smooth things over by offering new perspectives or helping find a middle ground.

In wrapping up, it's clear that talking about money in a blended family involves much more than just numbers. It's about sharing values, setting sights on future goals together, and building strong family relationships. These conversations are stepping stones to a solid financial foundation and a future where everyone in the family supports each other through ups and downs. The journey doesn't stop with a good financial plan. It continues as the family grows, always revisiting and evolving their strategies to ensure they work for everyone, shaping a future filled with shared success and unity.

Comprehensive Guide to Blended Family Success

ESSENTIAL STRATEGIES FOR SMOOTH TRANSITIONS, MASTERING CO-PARENTING, AND CREATING A COHESIVE, JOYFUL HOME

"Blended families are woven together by choice, strengthened together by love, tested by everything, and each uniquely ours."

Unknown

Hey there!

I'm your guide on this exciting journey through the world of blended families. Not too long ago, I was like you, navigating the ups and downs of bringing two families together. I know firsthand how challenging and rewarding it can be. With this book, I aim to make the path smoother for you, offering practical advice and heartfelt support at every step.

I have a favor to ask that won't take much of your time but can make a huge difference to someone else. Can you help someone you've never met by leaving a review of this book?

Think about how much easier it would be for others like you—remarried adults, stepparents, and kids in blended families—if they had the guidance and support they needed. Your review can help them find this resource and navigate their blended family journey confidently and joyfully.

Here's why your review matters:

- It can help one more family find peace and happiness.

- It can guide one more parent through the challenges of blending families.
- It can make the journey easier for one more person looking for support.

Leaving a review costs nothing and takes less than a minute, but it can change someone's life. Your review could be why someone finds the advice and encouragement they need.

To leave a review, just scan the QR code below:

If you enjoy helping others, you're exactly who I'm looking to connect with. Welcome to the community! I'm excited to help you navigate your remarriage journey and can't wait to share strategies to strengthen your relationship.

Thank you from the bottom of my heart. Now, back to our regularly scheduled programming.

Your biggest fan,

Taylor Reed

P.S. Sharing valuable advice makes you a key part of someone else's journey. Please pass this book on if you believe it will benefit another family.

SIX

Integrating Children and Teens into the Blended Family

In a blended family, kids often figure out where they fit in, filled with hope, adjustment, and sometimes confusion. Their emotions must be noticed, taken seriously, and understood. Integrating a family is a careful process where everything you say and do can bring people closer together or push them further apart.

Understanding How Kids Feel in a Blended Family

Recognizing Adjustment Periods

Adjustment periods for kids remind us that changes take time. Just like it takes a while for seasons to change, kids need time to get used to new family dynamics. Their adjustment can be unpredictable, lasting different amounts of time and feeling more intense for some than others. It's important to be patient during these times, offering a steady presence that helps them feel secure and reminding them that no difficult phase lasts forever.

Validating Feelings

Kids have a lot of feelings, and sometimes, adults try to soothe them without really getting how deep those feelings are. When we validate a child's emotions, we recognize they're real and matter and accept them without any strings attached. For example, if a kid is sad because they miss how things used to be at their old house, it's not helpful to just brush that off and discuss the new situation. Instead, acknowledging that they feel a sense of loss shows you hear them and care. It's like paying attention to them when they need it.

Providing Support Systems

Support systems like counseling and peer support groups are beneficial for kids dealing with tough emotions. These resources offer extra support, giving kids new ways to handle things that the family might be unable to provide alone. Think about a school counselor who can help a child express feelings they're struggling to put into words or a support group where they meet other kids going through similar family changes. This shows them they're not alone in what they're facing.

Encouraging Expression

Helping kids express their emotions can take more than just talking. Art is a great way to show their feelings, using colors and shapes to reveal what's inside. Journaling is another good method, giving them a private place to write down their thoughts. Having conversations that move at their speed can also help them feel more comfortable opening up. These methods are tools that help kids bring their feelings out into the open, making it easier for us to understand and connect with them.

Visual Element: Emotional Expression Toolkit

The emotional expression toolkit is a big help for kids to share their feelings. It might include art supplies for drawing out emotions, a journal with prompts about family changes, and conversation starters to get them talking about what they're going through. This guide allows parents to use these tools effectively, helping them be practical and sensitive as they help their kids express themselves and work through the challenges of becoming a blended family.

In a blended family, handling kids' emotions with care is crucial. Families can build a strong foundation of emotional intelligence and mutual respect by paying attention to how kids adjust, acknowledging their feelings, providing strong support, and encouraging different ways to express themselves. The Emotional Expression Toolkit is designed to help in this process. It gives kids ways to talk about their feelings and creates an environment where all emotions are an important part of the family's journey.

Teens in Blended Families: Individuality and Inclusion

Navigating the complex emotional worlds of teenagers in a blended family takes a careful approach that balances their need for independence with their need to feel included. Recognizing teenagers' need for privacy and space is key. As they stand on the brink of adulthood, teenagers are figuring out how to be independent while still wanting to feel connected to their family. This makes it important for parents and stepparents to respect their personal spaces, like bedrooms and online spaces, unless there are safety concerns. This kind of respect builds trust and shows that you see them as young adults, which can boost their self-esteem and mutual respect.

At the same time, including teenagers in family decisions is a great way to show them that their opinions matter. Whether deciding what to have for dinner or planning a family trip, giving them a say helps them feel more in control and teaches them about compromise and balancing different needs. These experiences prepare them for adulthood and make them feel valued within the family.

Teenagers in blended families might also struggle with their identity, trying to figure out how they fit into the new family picture while holding onto their backgrounds. Having open discussions about family history and the contributions of each family member can help them feel more connected and less isolated.

It's also crucial to support teenagers' lives outside the home. Friendships and activities like sports or clubs play a big part in their development. Encouraging these connections helps them maintain stability despite family changes and supports their emotional health.

Blended families can navigate the challenges together by encouraging their individuality and making them feel part of the family. This journey has no end point; it's about growing together, understanding each other better, and creating a supportive and accepting family environment. Regardless of age, every family member feels valued and important to the family's story.

Dealing with Sibling Rivalry in Blended Families

Sibling rivalry is common in blended families, and it's not unusual. It can stir up some trouble but also allows kids to grow closer. This rivalry often comes from kids feeling like they're competing for their parent's attention and resources. These feelings might not always be obvious, but they show up in how siblings interact, sometimes leading to envy, competition, or resentment. To handle this, it's crucial to create a fair environment where each child feels seen and valued equally, no matter where they stand in the family.

Fairness in a blended family ensures no one kid's needs overshadow another's. It means sharing your time and attention to show you care about everyone's needs, even if they're not all the same. Simple things like taking turns attending each child's events or making a big deal out of every child's achievements can help each kid feel they have a special place in the family. This helps reduce rivalry by showing that all kids are important to the family.

Handling sibling squabbles involves more than just telling them to get along. It's about teaching them how to deal with conflicts by understanding and respecting each other's feelings. Skills like expressing themselves without blaming, listening to understand, and finding compromises are key. Practicing these skills through role-playing can prepare them for real-life arguments, turning potential fights into chances to connect more deeply.

Celebrating each kid's achievements is another way to build a supportive family atmosphere. Whether it's a good grade, a sports win, or a cool art project, making a big deal out of these moments helps pull the family together. Everyone's successes boost the whole family, reducing the urge to compete for attention.

Building harmonious sibling relationships in blended families takes thoughtful and caring effort. By understanding the roots of rivalry, ensuring everyone is treated fairly, teaching kids how to handle disputes, and celebrating their successes, parents and stepparents can help siblings appreciate each other more. This approach doesn't just smooth over the challenges; it turns them into opportunities to strengthen the family bond, making it stronger and more supportive for everyone.

Strengthening Individual Family Bonds

In a blended family, focusing on each relationship is essential, ensuring everyone feels valued as an individual and part of the family. Spending one-on-one time with each child isn't just nice; it's crucial. This special time helps strengthen the connections and makes sure everyone feels important and included in the family.

Scheduling Regular One-on-One Time

Starting regular one-on-one time between a parent and child, or step-parent and stepchild, shows the family's dedication to building strong personal bonds. This practice recognizes each child's unique needs, interests, and feelings. It means making time in our busy lives for these important moments. Even though these moments might be short, they add up over time and create a strong foundation of trust and understanding. Whether it's a scheduled weekly hangout or grabbing the chance to connect whenever you can, these times are special opportunities to focus on each other, away from all other distractions.

Tailoring Activities to Interests

In these special one-on-one times, choosing activities that match the child's interests helps bring you closer, especially after all the changes and adjustments in a blended family. Whether going to the library together because you love books or hitting the trails for a hike because you're into the outdoors, these activities show you care. They tell the child that you see and value what they're passionate about. This makes them feel recognized and appreciated as individuals within the family.

Encouraging Open Dialogue

During these activities, having open conversations allows kids to share their thoughts and concerns freely. This kind of dialogue needs patience and careful listening, letting the child set the pace of the conversation. It's all about truly listening, where the responses from the parent or stepparent are thoughtful and not just quick fixes or judgments. By asking questions that help dig a bit deeper, you encourage the child to reflect and express themselves. Over time, this practice of open dialogue becomes a reliable way for kids to work through their feelings and thoughts, knowing they have someone who will listen and understand.

Strengthening Stepparent Relationships

Setting aside one-on-one time between stepparents and stepchildren in blended families is important. Building trust and a connection can be more challenging without the natural bond that comes with biological relationships. These one-on-one moments allow both to get to know each other, discover what they have in common and learn to appreciate their differences. Over time, as they build trust and understanding, the strength of their relationship becomes more apparent, deeply rooted in the experiences they share and the genuine care they develop for each other. These personal times are crucial for building strong, lasting bonds.

Balancing individual attention with overall family time is key in blended families. Regularly scheduling one-on-one time, choosing activities that align with personal interests, encouraging open conversations, and strengthening relationships between stepparents and stepchildren are all important. This approach ensures each child feels noticed, listened to, and valued for who they are. By doing this, families build stronger, more resilient relationships where everyone feels cared for and contributes to the family's overall harmony and strength.

Encouraging Openness: Kids' Perspectives on Blending Families

In blended families, everyone wants to be heard, especially the kids. It's crucial to create spaces where they can freely express themselves, sharing their thoughts, dreams, and worries about the new family setup. These can be formal, like a family meeting at the dinner table or casual chats during a car ride. Kids know their opinions are important in these safe spaces and feel empowered to shape the family's story.

Recognizing and validating kids' emotions is key. Whether they're happy or sad, every emotion they experience is important. Showing them their valid feelings, without making comparisons or setting conditions, helps them feel secure and respected in the family.

Listening to what kids have to say can change how adults see things. It's not about adults always leading; it's about sharing wisdom between generations. Paying attention to even the small stuff kids mention offers insights into their lives and helps parents adjust how the family works together. It's like tuning in to each child's detailed needs to ensure they all find their place.

Building empathy among family members turns a house into a home. Sharing stories about each person's past and present helps everyone understand each other better. This doesn't force everyone to be the same; instead, it highlights how each person's unique experiences and feelings contribute to the family.

In this environment of openness, children's voices are clear and strong. They help shape the family's understanding and empathy, enriching their life together. This isn't just about logistics; it's about building deep, emotional connections that make up a truly integrated family. In this way, blending a family becomes less of a task and more of a collective work of art, with every member, especially the kids, playing a crucial role.

Fostering a Sense of Belonging for Every Family Member

Creating an inclusive family identity means that every action, decision, and word is a step toward unity and belonging. The key is to see the family not just as a group of individuals who happen to live together but as a united team, made stronger by each member's contributions. This requires a strong commitment to building a shared identity that connects everyone deeply.

Start by identifying and nurturing shared values and goals. These values and goals form the foundation and direction of the family. Finding common values involves open communication, understanding what motivates each person, and seeing how these can blend into a unified vision. This process helps create a set of shared values where each one represents a commitment to living together as a family despite differences.

At the heart of this shared identity is celebrating these very differences. Each person's unique traits and experiences add to the family's richness. Recognizing and valuing these differences isn't just about acknowledging that they exist; it's about truly appreciating how they make the family stronger and more interesting. It shows that although the paths that brought each person to the family might differ, they all add valuable chapters to the family's overall story.

Creating a supportive environment is like building a haven filled with understanding, acceptance, and unconditional support. Here, everyone, no matter their role or background, can be themselves and grow without fear of judgment. This environment is built on active listening, empathy, and providing each person with the right support. It's a place where everyone's vulnerabilities are met with kindness, challenges are tackled together, and achievements are joyously celebrated. In this nurturing space, the family doesn't just survive; it thrives, knowing they are part of a caring and protective unit.

All these efforts—crafting an inclusive family identity, nurturing shared values, celebrating individuality, and creating a supportive atmosphere—wrap everyone in a sense of belonging. In this family fabric, regardless of how they came into the family, each person finds their special place of acceptance, understanding, and support. At the family's core, they are essential to its identity and growth.

As we wrap up this idea, it's clear that building a blended family where everyone truly belongs is both a careful process and a conscious effort. It involves celebrating each person's uniqueness and creating a shared identity that ties everyone together. Through this process, the family becomes a unified group, rich in diversity and united in their commitment to support and appreciate each other. This solid foundation of belonging helps the family handle the complexities of blended family life, confident in their strong bonds and shared future.

SEVEN

Building a Unified Family Culture

F amily traditions play a significant role in bringing blended families together in the hustle and bustle of everyday life, where routines set the pace and interactions fill our days. These traditions are more than just regular activities; they're the shared experiences that help bond the family as one. Creating and blending these traditions is important—it shows the family's dedication to sticking together, being inclusive, and respecting each other.

Establishing New Family Traditions That Honor All Members

Combining and Creating Traditions

Merging lives and histories in a blended family means mixing old traditions with new ones, which can be a fun and creative way to connect. Imagine a weekend where everyone gathers in the kitchen to cook together. Each person brings a special dish to them, and at the same time, everyone tries out some new recipes. This cooking session does more than just fill everyone up; it's a way for the family to honor each other's backgrounds while building new, shared experiences.

Inclusive Planning Process

Planning family traditions means ensuring everyone gets a say, from the youngest kid's fun ideas to the older members' wise suggestions. Picture the family sitting around the living room, maybe with a whiteboard in the middle, tossing ideas like they're in a lively brainstorming session. Every suggestion is taken seriously and considered respectfully. This team approach makes everyone feel part of shaping the family's culture. It shows how much each person's input is valued, helping to create a mix of traditions that represents what the family is all about.

Celebrating Diversity

In a world where differences can separate people, families can be places where everyone's unique backgrounds are celebrated, not just accepted. Traditions in a family mix all sorts of cultural, religious, and personal quirks, turning things like holidays and everyday routines into real expressions of shared life. For example, think about blending Hanukkah and Christmas, where lighting the menorah goes hand in hand with decorating the Christmas tree, or combining Diwali and Thanksgiving to make a festival of lights that brings out the meaning of gratitude. This shows how awesome it can be when different traditions come together.

Flexibility in Traditions

As families change over time, their traditions must also evolve, adapting to new circumstances with flexibility. This isn't about being less committed; it's about staying open to growth and change. For example, as kids get older or new members join the family, the yearly camping trip might shift from a roughing-it style to staying in cabins. This way, regardless of age or ability, everyone can still enjoy and be part of the fun and bonding. Being willing to adjust traditions like this helps keep them meaningful and inclusive, reflecting the family's evolving needs.

Visual Element: Tradition Brainstorming Whiteboard

Use a Tradition Brainstorming Whiteboard as a cool way to keep track of how you're creating and blending family traditions. Imagine a board with photos, doodles, and notes from all your family planning sessions. It's a fun visual reminder of everyone working together to shape family traditions. Plus, you could have a guide hanging next to it with tips on how to make these sessions engaging, inclusive, and creative. This makes the whole process more interesting and provides a handy tool for families to learn how to incorporate their unique traditions.

In the life of a blended family, family traditions act like strong pillars that help build a sense of unity and belonging. These traditions come from a process that respects everyone's background, cherishes traditions, and looks forward to creating future memories together. With an approach that embraces everyone's input, adapts over time, and celebrates the family's diverse backgrounds, you keep building a family culture that's rich and cohesive. In this way, the family becomes more than just the sum of its parts; it continuously evolves and always focuses on staying united and loving.

The Power of Family Rituals in Building Identity

Rituals are important in a blended family. They give everyone a sense of stability and belonging. These rituals, whether they happen every day or once a week, are more than just routines. They're meaningful practices that help strengthen the family's bond, creating a strong sense of unity that makes everyday life more memorable.

Daily and Weekly Rituals

In everyday life, rituals are what keep a family's rhythm going. Take the morning huddle, for example. It's just a quick moment when everyone catches up over breakfast before the day starts. In the morning rush, everyone shares what's up for the day and any worries, and they enjoy being together for a bit. Then there's the weekly family dinner, which is more relaxed than your typical weekday meal. Everyone comes together around a table full of homemade dishes, and this setting opens up space for longer chats, lots of laughs, and meaningful, quiet moments. These meals help bring everyone closer, bonding over every bite and shared story.

Rituals as Connection Points

These rituals are crucial for keeping family members connected amid their busy lives and personal challenges. They carve out special moments from busy schedules to strengthen family ties. For example, a nightly bedtime story goes beyond just reading about adventures and magic; it's a cherished time for closeness, a break from the day's hustle where you can share a quiet, comforting moment. Similarly, a Sunday hike gets everyone outside together, providing a chance to chat and explore, which helps build strong relationships like the paths you walk on.

Creating Meaningful Rituals

Starting these rituals requires tuning into what makes your family unique and finding what resonates with everyone. It might be about making music together, where nights are spent singing or playing instruments as a family. It could also be quieter, like keeping a shared journal where everyone writes about their thoughts and dreams. It is important to create these rituals together, ensuring they reflect what your family stands for and cares about. This turns them from regular routines into meaningful practices that strengthen your family's identity.

Adapting Rituals Over Time

As a family grows and changes, so do the rituals that mark their days and weeks. It's all about adapting—maybe the weekly movie night shifts from kids' cartoons to more grown-up documentaries as everyone ages. This keeps the rituals fresh and relevant, reflecting everyone's growing interests and changing perspectives.

These big or small rituals help the family find its special rhythm, creating a sense of connection, identity, and belonging. They are the moments everyone returns to, helping to tie everyone together as they move through life. They offer comfort and a sense of shared history and future, reassuring everyone that they're on this journey together, anchored by traditions that evolve with them.

Celebrating Milestones and Successes Together

In a blended family, celebrating milestones and successes brings everyone together, highlighting personal achievements and shared victories. These celebrations help mark the family's journey, reinforcing the connections and growth along the way. From birthdays and graduations to anniversaries and special achievements, these moments are key points that remind everyone about the family's journey and the bonds that tie them together.

Creating special traditions around these events makes them even more meaningful. Imagine having a family tradition where every graduation, whether from preschool or college, includes not just a party and gifts but also adding to a family book filled with messages of wisdom, encouragement, and love from everyone. This kind of tradition links generations and tells the family's ongoing story.

It's also important to ensure these celebrations include something from everyone's background, especially in a blended family. For instance, adding cultural or religious elements meaningful to a new stepsibling's birthday can show real respect and welcome them fully into the family. This way, family celebrations add to the family's story and respect and embrace everyone's unique contributions.

These shared celebrations do more than just mark another year or achievement; they strengthen family ties and affirm the family's collective values and identity. Think about having a family day each year dedicated to celebrating being a family, where everyone might work on a project together, like starting a garden or sharing their hopes and dreams. These traditions are not just events; they're important connections to the heart of the family, boosting everyone's sense of belonging and shared purpose.

The Importance of Flexibility in Family Life

In a blended family, things are always changing, and it takes a special kind of toughness to keep up. You have to be able to adjust and be flexible as family dynamics shift, kids grow, and relationships evolve. It's like being able to roll with the punches and adapt as things change around you.

Embracing Change

In family life, change isn't something to fight against; it's actually on your side, helping you grow and get closer if you're open to it. While it's natural to want to stick to the way things used to be, learning to embrace change can open up many opportunities. When a family adjusts to new situations and grows to include new ideas or people, it strengthens the ties between everyone. It's not so much about getting lost in all the changes as it is about finding new ways to connect once things settle down and, in the process, discovering deeper levels of love and understanding.

Adapting to Individual Growth

As each person in the family grows and changes, the whole family dynamic shifts. A child who used to hold tightly to a parent's hand might now be stepping confidently into their teen years, changing their role in the family. It becomes essential to adjust to these changes, figuring out when to give support and space. The family must find a balance, providing enough support to catch someone if they fall and enough freedom to let them grow. This flexibility allows everyone to grow individually while keeping the family strong and unified, ensuring no one's journey gets lost.

Flexibility in Traditions and Rituals

Traditions and rituals are essential to family life but can change over time to better suit the family's needs. For example, if Sunday dinners used to be your thing, but schedules change and interests shift, you might switch to shared morning walks instead. This change in tradition isn't about losing something; it's more about giving these practices new life. It's important to remember that the value of these traditions isn't just in doing the same thing the same way all the time. Still, in the meaning behind them—they're meant to bring everyone together, not hold anyone back, letting each family member find new ways to connect as the family grows and changes.

Communicating Through Transitions

Good communication is at the heart of handling change, acting like a safety net to ensure no one feels left out or misunderstood. The family can stick together through changes by openly sharing thoughts, fears, and hopes, ensuring everyone is heard and comforted. Sometimes, this communication isn't just about talking; it can be a look or a simple touch that shows support and togetherness. It's a way to remind each other that the family is a steady place where everyone belongs no matter what changes come.

A blended family shows its strength in adapting and being flexible. This strength doesn't come from being rigid but from being willing to adjust and go with the flow, finding ways around challenges and bringing new energy to family life. This adaptability gives the family the resilience they need to handle the ups and downs of life together, turning each change into an opportunity to grow closer and understand each other better.

Blending Family Histories: Sharing Stories

In a blended family, everyone—no matter how different they might seem—brings something special to the table, adding to the family's overall vibe. Sharing each person's history and stories is crucial. It's not just about telling what happened in the past; it's about building a deeper understanding and empathy among everyone. This act of sharing turns regular moments into opportunities for connection, helping to knit the family together through their shared experiences and collective background.

Sharing Individual Histories

Imagine a quiet evening when the family comes together, putting aside TVs and phones and just sitting under the warm light of a lamp to share stories from their lives. Here, a stepfather might talk about his childhood adventures in far-off places, bringing everyone into his past world, which might differ from theirs. Then, a teenager might talk about her own experiences, like changing schools, and her stories of resilience might strike a chord with her younger siblings. Making this storytelling a regular thing turns it into more than just swapping memories. It becomes a special time when everyone can be open about their feelings, appreciate their differences, and find things they have in common, bringing everyone closer with each story they share.

Creating a Shared Family Narrative

As family members share their stories from the past, they all start working together to weave a shared family story that includes bits from everyone's history. This rich, diverse narrative becomes the base of the family's identity. Everyone shares their own experiences, and these stories are woven together to celebrate the journey of becoming a blended family. Through blending these past and present tales, the family creates its unique voice, showing the strength and beauty of its unity.

Honoring Past and Present

When blending family histories, respecting the past and present is essential. Recognizing everyone's journeys, full of ups and downs, is key to building the family's story together. One way might be to create a wall of memories where photos and keepsakes from everyone's life are displayed. This shows off each person's unique path alongside the family's shared experiences. Also, making a point to celebrate special dates important to individual members—like remembering a loved one's passing or celebrating a cultural holiday—just as enthusiastically as you would a family birthday or anniversary helps reinforce that everyone's background is important and valued. This approach of blending the past and present reminds the family that while they are moving forward, the individual stories that brought them here are treasured parts of their shared identity.

Documenting Family Milestones

Keeping track of milestones and stories in a blended family is super important. It helps keep memories alive and guides future generations. You can do this by making scrapbooks full of photos and keepsakes or creating digital albums to capture those quick, fleeting moments of family life. Each item, like a kid's drawing of their new family or a parent's thoughts on blending lives, adds to the family's history, keeping the details of their journey alive for years. This kind of project gets everyone involved, making documenting another way for the family to share experiences. As you fill up pages or add to your digital galleries, the family's story gets told in rich detail, showing off the challenges they've overcome, the happy moments they've celebrated, and the strong connections they've built.

Blending family histories helps shape the family's identity. The family crafts its unique story by sharing personal stories, creating a shared narrative, respecting both past and present, and documenting important moments. This story, built on empathy, understanding, and respect, highlights the importance of accepting and celebrating each person's journey. Ultimately, these shared stories create a sense of belonging and a reminder of the love and unity that holds the family together.

The Journey Forward: Evolving as a Blended Family

Creating a vision for the future in a blended family involves shared dreams and goals. This vision guides the family through life's ups and downs. It requires everyone to align their desires with the family's overall objectives, ensuring everyone's aspirations fit the bigger picture. This vision evolves with each success and challenge, constantly reshaped by the family's experiences and growth.

Focusing on continual growth and learning is vital. This principle recognizes that family life is ever-changing and full of discoveries. It's about pursuing knowledge together through educational activities or exploring new places and cultures. Every day offers opportunities to learn more about the world and each other, making growth and learning a core part of the family's identity.

Throughout this journey, the family's resilience is tested and strengthened. Building resilience means creating an environment where everyone feels supported. This involves open discussions about challenges and fears, fostering mutual support and understanding. Families share and develop coping strategies, like mindfulness practices or physical activities, to reduce stress and increase well-being. This resilience helps the family navigate the complexities of blended family life confidently.

Celebrating milestones and successes is important. These moments allow the family to reflect on their journey, recognize their growth, and appreciate each other. Celebrations, whether big or small, reinforce the family's bond and achievements, adding to their ongoing story of resilience, love, and unity.

The family feels anticipation and hope when Looking to the future. The vision they've crafted together, along with the lessons learned and resilience built, lights the way forward. As they move into the next chapter of their lives, they know they can face whatever the future holds together.

In this journey of growth and evolution, the blended family finds true togetherness. Their bond is strengthened through shared goals, learning, and celebrating their collective journey. Though unique to them, this journey echoes the universal themes of love, resilience, and the enduring power of family.

EIGHT

Transforming Blended Family Dynamics

Blended families get their strength and unique character from their diversity. However, feelings of alienation can sometimes emerge, subtly but deeply. Making sure no one feels like an outsider requires deliberate actions that create an environment where everyone is included and accepted.

Strategies for Inclusion

Encouraging Open Dialogue

Creating a culture where everyone feels heard can start simply at the dinner table. It's a daily spot where everyone comes together, and honest conversations happen amid passing dishes and clinking glasses. People talk about their fears, their dreams, and just everyday stuff. It's a comfortable place where family members can talk about feeling left out without worrying about being judged. Whether it's a teenager discussing the awkwardness of a new school or a stepparent talking about fitting in, these dinner talks help everyone better understand and support each other.

Designating Specific Family Roles

Giving each family member specific roles or tasks isn't just about dividing up chores; it's about making everyone feel important and connected. Whether it's keeping track of the family calendar or picking out movies for movie night, these roles help each person see how they contribute to the family, making them feel needed and valued. For example, letting kids plan their weekend activities boosts their confidence and shows that their ideas and preferences matter, making them feel like a crucial part of the family.

Creating Inclusive Family Activities

Imagine spending a Saturday with the family working together on a fun project, like starting a garden in the backyard. This kind of activity is great because it appeals to all ages, and everyone can pitch in, whether picking out what to plant or gardening. Working together like this builds a sense of belonging, as everyone can see the results of their hard work grow over time. Choosing activities like this helps bring the family closer, allowing everyone to contribute, learn, and have fun together, making any divisions feel less important.

Regular Check-Ins

One-on-one check-ins are powerful because they're so simple. A walk with a stepchild, a drive to the store, or just a quiet moment before bed can turn into a chance for a meaningful chat. These quick check-ins provide a private moment for someone to share worries or achievements that might get overlooked in a group setting. They're an excellent time to bring up and address any feelings of being left out, making sure everyone knows that no issue is too small to talk about. Regularly making these check-ins builds trust, showing every family member that their feelings and experiences matter.

Visual Element: Inclusion Checklist

An Inclusion Checklist can be a handy tool for families to implement these strategies. This checklist is easy to use and lays out daily and weekly actions to help everyone feel included, like making sure each family member gets a turn to speak at dinner or setting up regular one-on-one check-ins. It also includes prompts for reflection so families can see how well their efforts are working and make adjustments if needed. This makes the process of fostering inclusion active and adaptable.

In managing the complexities of a blended family, addressing feelings of being left out requires thoughtful strategies that make everyone feel like they belong. Open conversations, assigning specific family roles, planning activities that include everyone, and regular personal check-ins are key ways to ensure no one feels left out. With tools like the Inclusion Checklist, these ideas can be implemented effectively, helping families weave together a supportive and unified environment where every member is important and feels connected.

Managing Ex-Partner Relations: Building Cooperation

Dealing with ex-partners can be tricky when working with a blended family. It's all about finding the right balance and managing tension while keeping things cooperative. The goal isn't to forget all the past issues but to build a setting where everyone communicates clearly and treats each other respectfully. Getting this balance right helps ensure that the kids stay the main focus without any adult disagreements getting in the way.

Establishing Clear Boundaries

Setting clear boundaries with ex-partners is critical to smoothly managing a blended family. It's about clearly defining each parent's roles and responsibilities in the kids' lives and ensuring everyone sticks to these rules. This helps keep personal conflicts out of the way of co-parenting. For instance, agreeing on how and when parents and stepparents will communicate sets a respectful path for everyone involved. Keeping conversations focused on the kids' needs and activities rather than personal details strengthens this approach even more. This way, the co-parenting relationship respects everyone's space and keeps the focus on raising the children.

Developing a Co-Parenting Plan

Creating a co-parenting plan is a practical step forward, setting out a clear strategy for how you'll raise the kids together. This plan details everything from daily routines to how you'll handle schooling, medical care, and holidays. It's a joint effort that requires honest conversation and some give-and-take, ensuring each parent's views are heard and included in a unified approach. If you treat this plan as something that can be updated as things change and the kids grow, it becomes a handy tool. It helps minimize disagreements and keeps both households aligned on what's best for the kids.

Using Mediation Services

Mediation can be a great way to find some middle ground when co-parents struggle to talk things out directly. Mediators are trained in helping people resolve conflicts, and they create a structured setting where both parties can work through their issues. While it might feel like you're admitting you can't communicate well, using a mediator shows that both parents are serious about keeping their co-parenting relationship functional. The mediator's office becomes a place where you can work through past issues and current disagreements, coming to agreements that show compromise, respect, and a shared focus on what's best for the kids.

Focusing on Positive Communication

The key to all these strategies is just good communication. This means focusing on giving helpful feedback, really listening, and not throwing around blame. Positive communication shifts how you talk, aiming more for teamwork and less for pointing fingers over old issues. It takes some patience and a bit of stepping back to think about how you're expressing your concerns and needs in a way that builds understanding instead of getting everyone's back up. For example, if you frame requests around what's good for the kids—like saying, "It would mean a lot to [child's name] if..."—it comes off less like a critique and more like a joint goal, which makes cooperation easier.

By sticking to this approach, you create an environment where respectful and valuable conversations are the norm, setting up a co-parenting relationship based on mutual respect and teamwork. Navigating relationships with ex-partners in a blended family isn't just about following steps; it's about adopting a comprehensive approach that shifts from conflict to cooperation. Establishing clear boundaries, making a detailed co-parenting plan, using mediators when needed, and committing to positive communication aren't just actions but a full strategy to make co-parenting work. This focus on working together for the kids' benefit means that the path of the blended family isn't shadowed by past problems but is lit by collaborative efforts, creating a stable and supportive environment where kids can flourish.

Harmonizing Different Parenting Styles: Practical Tips and Tricks

Getting different parenting styles to work together in a blended family is tough. It's all about patience, understanding, and willingness to make changes to build a family atmosphere where everyone feels respected and loved. Finding common ground on how to raise the kids is crucial. It's not about big moves but starts with listening to each other—understanding their values, beliefs, and expectations. It's about working out where you agree and where you don't, treating these talks as a way to get where the other is coming from.

Once you've found common ground, you can start setting household rules and decide how to handle discipline. This step is like balancing being firm but also flexible. You outline clear boundaries and expectations that apply to all kids, no matter what. This part keeps evolving; you keep tweaking the rules to ensure they fit your family values and what you agree about parenting. Consistency in applying these rules is vital—it gives the kids a stable, predictable environment and shows a united front as parents.

Sometimes, getting outside help through parenting workshops or counseling can be a game changer. These resources are like getting expert navigation tips. They offer a structured way to learn new parenting techniques, get advice tailored to blended families, and hear from others facing similar challenges. This outside perspective can help you see compromise and cooperation opportunities that weren't obvious before.

Lastly, being flexible as your family grows and changes is essential. What works now might not work in a year, so being open to feedback and ready to adjust your methods is essential. This flexibility shows a mature approach to parenting—it's about evolving with your family's needs while keeping a consistent approach in front of the kids.

Blending lives and parenting styles in blended families is complex but rewarding. By finding common ground, setting clear rules, seeking outside guidance, and staying flexible, parents can create a parenting approach that honors each family member's individuality while building unity and respect. This effort sets the foundation for a family life filled with love, understanding, and cooperation, ultimately creating a harmonious family dynamic.

Financial Planning: Creating a Plan for Everyone

Handling finances in a blended family can get complicated. Everyone must come together to talk about money honestly and fairly. You'll need to figure out how to respect what each person can contribute while ensuring the whole family's needs are met. This is all about being transparent with each other, treating everyone equally, and working together. It's like figuring out the best way to navigate through different challenges and opportunities that pop up along the way.

Joint Financial Planning Sessions

Starting regular financial planning meetings allows family members to come together and tackle their money matters as a team. Marking these sessions as important recurring events on your calendar helps everyone stay on the same page. In these meetings, you lay everything out clearly—how much money is coming in, what the expenses are, and what everyone hopes to save up for, whether it's a new car or a family vacation.

Although the topic is serious, the meetings keep a team spirit. One person doesn't just decide how to budget, save, and spend; everyone gets a say, and the final plans reflect everyone's input. Spreadsheets, budgeting apps, and financial statements help make informed decisions. These tools aren't there to restrict you but to help you all work towards a future where financial worries are less of a burden and financial security is a straightforward goal within reach.

Equitable Contribution Plans

Figuring out how each family member can chip in financially is like balancing things just right. Everyone comes from different financial backgrounds, and this process respects that. It's not just about the money—each contribution shows commitment to the family. To create a fair system, you must consider different incomes, other money obligations, and personal needs. This doesn't mean everyone pays the same amount. It's about making sure that whether someone's contribution is money, time, or effort, it's all valued equally. This approach helps strengthen the family bond through mutual respect and appreciation.

Transparent Financial Communication

Talking openly about finances in a family is about building trust and being transparent with each other. It's more than just sharing how much everyone earns or spends; it's about discussing your hopes, fears, and money-related plans. Bringing up debts and financial responsibilities isn't easy, but handling these talks seriously is important to keep everyone on the same page. This openness helps avoid nasty financial surprises that could destroy family harmony. Keeping everything transparent creates a trust-filled environment where everyone can feel secure. This ongoing conversation is critical to managing finances smoothly and keeping the family on solid ground.

Professional Financial Advice

When finances get tricky—maybe due to inheritance issues, college savings, or investment choices—getting help from a professional financial advisor is smart. These experts know the ropes because they've helped others in similar situations, and they can offer advice that clears up any confusion. It's better to seek their guidance early rather than wait for overwhelming things. This helps the family make well-informed choices, whether planning for a child's education or buying a home for everyone.

A blended family can smoothly merge love and money by working together on a financial plan that considers everyone's needs, dreams, and what they can contribute. This approach makes financial planning a unifying activity rather than just a necessary chore, strengthening family ties and setting the stage for handling money matters confidently and successfully in the future.

Building Self-Esteem: Overcoming Comparison

In every blended family, relationships form a complex network where feelings of inadequacy and comparison can easily creep in. The key to overcoming these feelings isn't through big gestures but by creating a nurturing environment where everyone feels valued and affirmed.

Regular affirmations are crucial—small, consistent acts that help everyone feel appreciated. These might be supportive comments after a setback, a thank you note tucked into a pillow or praise for a small achievement. These acts help embed the message into everyday life that everyone is valued just as they are.

Highlighting each person's strengths and celebrating their achievements also plays a big role. It's about noticing and appreciating everyone's contributions, no matter how small, which helps build self-esteem. Celebrations don't have to be big—a laugh shared over a hidden talent, showing off a creative project or a quick toast to a personal win can all make a big impact.

Sometimes, though, affirmations and celebrations aren't enough when the feelings of inadequacy are deep-seated. That's where family counseling can help. Counseling provides a safe space to explore these feelings with professional guidance, helping everyone express themselves and find strategies to support each other better.

Building a culture of appreciation within the family is like setting up an environment where confidence can grow. It's about consciously focusing on the positive, daily recognizing efforts and successes, whether during dinner, family projects, or quiet evening chats. In this supportive atmosphere, unnecessary comparisons disappear, replaced by joy in seeing each other and oneself grow.

Navigating a blended family involves moving beyond comparing oneself to others through a steady practice of affirmation, celebration, and, when needed, professional counseling, all underpinned by a strong culture of appreciation. This approach helps everyone in the family feel recognized and valued for who they are, fostering an environment where self-esteem and confidence can blossom.

Celebrating Diversity: Integrating Cultures and Traditions

Bringing different cultures and traditions together in a family isn't just routine—it's a fantastic chance to create a shared identity that celebrates everyone's background. Imagine having Cultural Education Nights, where the family gathers to explore different cultures through stories, music, and food. One night might be about the rhythms of West Africa, another about South Asian spices, or the folk art of Eastern Europe. These nights aren't just educational; they connect everyone to the diverse experiences that shape our world, turning the living room into a fun, boundary-less classroom where curiosity leads to understanding and respect.

Being inclusive about holidays and celebrations ensures that every important day from any culture gets its moment in the spotlight. This might mean lighting Hanukkah candles one night and setting up a Christmas tree the next or blending the traditions of Eid with Easter practices to create new, unique family rituals. This approach ensures no one's heritage is left out but becomes a celebrated part of the family's life.

Working on cultural projects together adds another layer to this mix. Maybe it's making a quilt from fabrics representing each person's heritage or putting together a family cookbook with recipes from around the world. These projects are more than just fun activities; they represent the family's journey toward unity and respect, filled with shared laughter and learning.

Sometimes, blending such diverse backgrounds requires external help. Consulting with cultural experts or community leaders can help sensitively navigate these complexities. They can offer advice on everything from celebrating religious holidays respectfully to understanding cultural nuances, ensuring that the family's approach is thoughtful and genuine.

As this section wraps up, we see how cultural education, inclusive planning, joint projects, and expert advice help blended families integrate diverse cultures and traditions successfully. It's all about curiosity, respect, and celebrating each person's unique contribution to the family's collective identity. As we move forward, we understand that our differences are not just to be tolerated but celebrated, forming a vibrant, inclusive, and connected family foundation.

Next, we shift focus to communication—an essential aspect of any family life but especially crucial in the complex dynamics of a blended family. We'll explore strategies to ensure open, honest, and affectionate exchanges that help every family member feel heard and understood.

NINE

Integrating into the Blended Family

In a world where families are constantly changing, figuring out how to fit into a blended family can be complex. Each new family member adds their unique style to the mix. Making sure everyone blends well together takes some thoughtful effort. Mixing different lives and backgrounds is key to building a united family.

Finding Your Place in the Blended Family

Identifying Unique Contributions

Everyone brings their skills, experiences, and viewpoints to a blended family, creating a unique family identity. Creating a Family Talent Tree is a fun way to recognize and value everyone's contributions. Think of this tree as having different branches, each representing various strengths and interests—like artistic talents, problem-solving skills, empathy, leadership qualities, and more. Each family member can add a leaf to the branches where they think their strengths are. This creates a visual and hands-on way to celebrate what each person brings to the family.

Individual and Group Therapy

For anyone struggling to find their place in the family, therapy can be a big help, guiding them through the emotional ups and downs of blending families. Therapy can be one-on-one, giving someone a private place to figure themselves out, or with the whole family, where everyone can share their experiences and grow together. For example, a family might attend group therapy sessions to improve communication. These guided discussions help clear any misunderstandings and worries, helping everyone feel more connected.

Family Bonding Activities

Shared experiences are vital to building a strong family bond. Setting up regular family activities, like weekly board game nights, monthly hikes, or annual projects like building a treehouse, helps everyone feel connected. It's important to pick activities everyone can enjoy, regardless of their interests and abilities, to feel included and important. Imagine spending a Saturday together on a big art project where everyone adds their touch to a giant canvas, showing how all the different styles combine to create something beautiful.

Open Discussions About Roles

In a blended family, everyone has a unique role that contributes to the family's harmony. Holding open discussions about each person's role and how the family works together is crucial. These discussions should happen in an environment where everyone feels respected and can openly share their feelings, expectations, and concerns about their place in the family. An excellent way to do this could be to have a monthly Family Forum. Here, you can talk about anything from who does what chores to deeper issues like how everyone feels about their place and identity in the family.

Visual Element: The Family Talent Tree

Adding a Family Talent Tree to this chapter gives families a cool, interactive way to showcase and celebrate everyone's skills and interests. This activity comes with a tree template and leaves, making it easy for families to visualize what each person brings to the family. It also includes guidelines and discussion questions to help everyone explore and appreciate each other's unique contributions. The Family Talent Tree is more than just a fun craft; it's a great way to see and value each person's role in the family.

Dealing with the dynamics of a blended family means finding your spot in a complex mix of relationships and backgrounds. This chapter offers various strategies to help with that, from celebrating each person's input and getting professional advice to doing activities together and having open talks about family roles. Using these methods, blended families can turn the tough parts of coming together into chances to grow and strengthen their bonds, creating a vibrant and resilient family unit.

Tips for Unified Parenting

Parenting in a blended family is about working together, each bringing their own style and strengths. Starting regular parenting meetings is a significant first step. These aren't formal—just dedicated times to talk about how parenting is going, discuss strategies, and celebrate wins. Imagine sitting in the living room, maybe with a cup of tea, just talking things through in a supportive atmosphere.

Taking parenting classes that focus on the unique needs of blended families can also be super helpful. These classes offer tips and insights and provide a place to connect with others in similar situations. It's like having a classroom where you can laugh and learn together, easing tension and building bonds through shared experiences.

Another critical part is figuring out parenting roles that play to each person's strengths, almost like assigning parts in a play. This requires some give and take, but keeping the kids' well-being as the primary focus helps guide these decisions. The result? A co-parenting plan that feels balanced and fair.

Of course, it's not always smooth sailing. When challenges arise, leaning on external supports like family therapists or support groups is often helpful. These resources can provide valuable advice and reassurance, reminding you that you're not alone.

In the end, blending different parenting styles takes patience, willingness to learn, and a bit of creativity. Regular meetings, classes, sharing responsibilities, and getting outside help are steps toward a robust and unified approach to parenting. These efforts strengthen the family bond, creating a united front of collaboration, understanding, and respect.

Managing Money Together: A Guide to Financial Unity

Financial Planning Workshops

Attending financial planning workshops can strengthen how you understand and handle money as a family. These workshops are packed with useful information and tactics for managing finances together. Imagine a room where everyone's around tables filled with budgets, forecasts, and financial plans, all ready to be tailored to a blended family's needs. Led by experts who know the ins and outs of financial planning, families can get better at turning numbers into practical plans that match their shared goals. These sessions are a great way to lay the foundations for financial unity, with everyone committed to overcoming financial challenges and building a stable, prosperous future together.

Open Financial Discussions

We're working to create a home where talking about money is as easy as chatting over dinner, built on a solid base of trust and openness. In such an environment, discussing finances becomes a chance to connect and grow, not a cause for stress or arguments. This kind of space, where judgment is left at the door, and empathy is the norm, encourages everyone in the family to share their financial hopes, worries, and plans without holding back. Whether it's a teenager discussing college funds, a stepparent talking about retirement, or a younger child curious about the cost of their hobbies, every voice is heard and respected. These open conversations help build a deep understanding of finances across the family, marked by honesty and mutual respect, setting everyone up for a harmonious financial future.

Developing a Unified Financial Plan

Creating a solid financial plan for a blended family involves teamwork and looking ahead. It's not just about adding up what everyone earns and spends—imagining where you want to go together and making smart choices now to get there. Gathered around the table, you map out your goals, like owning a home, paying for education, traveling, and retiring. Each person pitches in, regardless of age, sharing their dreams and needs. It's about balancing what everyone wants and what's best for the whole family. Working together builds a strong foundation for a secure financial future, showing how unity can conquer even the trickiest money.

Setting Financial Boundaries

Setting financial boundaries in a blended family is like building a sturdy wall against money arguments that can mess with your family's harmony. It's all about finding the right balance—figuring out who's responsible for what and what you're all in on together. You must have those honest talks where you lay down the rules, set limits, and make agreements to keep personal spending separate from family stuff. It might feel awkward initially, but having a money relationship based on respect and understanding is worth it. Whether divvying up cash for hobbies or chipping into a family savings pot, it's about finding common ground and being considerate. By laying down these money boundaries, you're setting up a solid structure where financial peace isn't just a dream—it's the real deal, ensuring that managing money together doesn't drive you apart but brings you closer as a family.

Building Strong Step-Relationships

Building strong step-relationships is crucial in a blended family, and it all starts with creating a space where everyone feels heard and respected. This isn't just about being polite—it's about trying to understand each other, putting yourself in someone else's shoes, and seeing things from their perspective. By doing this, empathy becomes the main driver in family interactions, helping smooth out misunderstandings and fostering an environment where respect can thrive.

Handling conflicts well is another big part of making blended family life work. It's about preparing for disagreements with calmness and precision. Setting up clear ways to communicate and rules for discussions helps ensure that when disagreements happen, they can be dealt with constructively. Role-playing potential conflicts and attending workshops on negotiation and compromise are great ways to strengthen the family's ability to handle whatever comes up.

Balancing family time with personal time is like being a conductor who ensures every instrument plays its part harmoniously. Enjoying things together, like game nights or movie evenings, brings everyone closer. But it's also essential to respect each other's need for alone time, which adds depth to the family dynamics.

Celebrating small wins also plays a significant role in nurturing step-relationships. Whether it's a joke bringing a stepparent and stepsibling closer or getting through a tough conversation, recognizing these moments helps everyone see their progress. Regularly acknowledging these achievements, whether through a quick celebration or by keeping a "family wins" journal, helps build a positive atmosphere where every little step towards unity is celebrated.

The process of blending lives in blended families is complex but rewarding. It involves intentionally fostering respect and empathy, navigating conflicts wisely, finding the right mix of togetherness and individuality, and celebrating every small victory. Committing to these actions allows a blended family to coexist; it grows into a vibrant, united group where every member is valued and understood.

Dealing With the Past: Moving Forward Together

In a blended family, everyone brings past experiences into the mix. It's important to acknowledge and understand these past experiences, like looking at an old map and seeing where everyone has come from. In the safe space of the family, there's room to share these stories and learn from them, which can help everyone feel more connected and understood.

Building new, positive memories together is also crucial. Whether laughing over a spontaneous dance-off in the kitchen or sharing a quiet moment under the stars, these new experiences help strengthen family bonds and build a sense of togetherness. They lay the foundation for new memories that enrich the family's shared story.

Forgiveness and letting go of past grievances are also crucial. This often involves honest conversations in which apologies are made, wounds are cared for, and forgiveness is freely offered. These steps are crucial for moving past old hurts and toward a future that does not weigh them down.

Keeping open lines of communication is the thread that ties all this together. It ensures that past issues don't linger and that everyone feels heard. Regular chats at the dinner table or during a family meeting help maintain transparency and build trust.

A blended family can navigate the complexities of their unique dynamics by actively working on understanding the past, creating new memories, practicing forgiveness, and keeping communication open. This approach helps them deal with the past, celebrate their present, and look forward to their future together.

Making It Work: Strategies for Long-Term Success

In a blended family, each member brings unique qualities and a shared commitment, lighting the way toward lasting harmony and success. Setting long-term goals together is critical, and it requires everyone's input, working not just as a group thrown together but as a team to build a future on their combined dreams and realities. From these meetings, clear goals take shape that everyone can work towards.

While it's essential to be realistic, dreaming big is also part of the process. Balancing daily needs with bigger dreams ensures the family plans for an exciting and attainable future. These plans become living proof of the family's strength, adaptability, and commitment to each other.

Celebrating milestones is more than just marking achievements; it's about recognizing the family's perseverance and unity. Whether a small gathering or a big celebration, these moments are a chance to reflect, appreciate, and motivate everyone to keep growing together. These celebrations highlight progress and infuse the family's journey with purpose.

Blended families must stay flexible, adapting to changes and their members' evolving needs. This openness to change keeps the family dynamic solid and capable of overcoming new challenges. Embracing change as part of growth helps keep everyone connected and moving forward.

Support from outside the family, like therapy or support groups, plays a crucial role. These resources offer new perspectives and strategies, providing comfort and empowerment. They remind the family that they're not alone, strengthening their bonds through shared knowledge and support from the wider community.

Strategies like setting joint goals, celebrating milestones, staying adaptable, and seeking external support are vital for managing the blend of past experiences, current realities, and future hopes. They guide the family toward turning today's challenges into tomorrow's victories and embracing the complex, beautiful journey of creating a connected, joyful family life. As the family moves forward, they continue weaving a story that reflects their unique path and the universal search for belonging and love.

TEN

Blended Family Strategies: Everyday Solutions

Navigating blended family life can feel like trying to solve a puzzle without being able to see the pieces. Every decision shuffles things around, but finding the right fit is hard. When the complexities of living as a blended family start to feel overwhelming, having specific solutions for different situations can be a game-changer. Instead of stumbling around, these tailored strategies can light up the issues, helping you discover patterns and approaches that lead to a smoother family life.

Tailored Solutions for Real-Life Challenges

Tailored Guidance

Blended families are different, each with a mix of personalities, backgrounds, and challenges. A one-size-fits-all approach doesn't cut it for their complex needs. Instead, solutions must be as unique and flexible as the families themselves. Take the task of creating new family traditions, for example. It might seem easy to mix traditions from both sides, but this can sometimes make people feel like their family's ways are getting lost or overshadowed. A better approach might be to start new traditions that borrow elements from both families while adding something new. This way, you honor everyone's past and build a sense of unity and a shared identity for the future.

Real-Life Scenarios

Using real examples can turn vague advice into something practical and valuable. Let's examine how different parenting styles might clash in a blended family. Imagine a stepmom used to a strict routine moves in with her partner, who is more laid-back with his kids. Tensions might flare up when it comes to bedtimes and homework rules. A practical solution could be holding a "family summit" where kids talk about what they prefer and what bothers them. From this meeting, they could create a Family Charter, which would spell out rules and routines that mix both the strict and lenient styles, aiming for a middle ground that everyone can agree on.

Adaptability of Solutions

Families change over time, and solutions that were great a while back might not cut it anymore. Being flexible is crucial. One way to stay adaptable is to have regular "family check-ins." These are times when everyone can discuss what's going well and what's not. These check-ins help you monitor how the family is doing and adjust your approach. For example, a weekly meeting that used to focus on chores and schedules might shift to every other week, with more emphasis on how everyone is feeling and strengthening family bonds as you all grow closer together.

Problem-Solving Framework

A structured way to solve problems gives families a clear path to handle challenges confidently. This method has four simple steps: Identify, Discuss, Plan, and Review. First, the family pinpoints the problem, like a disagreement about screen time or how to celebrate holidays. Then, everyone gets a chance to talk about it openly. After that, the family works together to devise a plan, set clear goals, and decide who is responsible for what. Lastly, they look back at how things went, figuring out what worked well and what might need some tweaking. This approach tackles the immediate issues and helps strengthen the family's problem-solving ability.

Visual Element: The Family Problem-Solving Chart

Something like the Family Problem-Solving Chart can help families see and work through their issues more clearly. This chart visually lays out the steps to tackle problems, with specific sections for each part of the process. Along with the chart are "scenario cards" that show common challenges blended families might face, providing a way to talk through and practice solving these issues. This setup isn't just great for sorting out conflicts; it's also a helpful way to teach families how to handle future problems more smoothly.

This chapter provides practical advice designed explicitly for blended families' unique situations. From starting new traditions and mixing different parenting styles to staying flexible and using a straightforward problem-solving method, the goal is to help families improve their understanding and cooperation. With tools like the Problem-Solving Chart and tailored solutions for real-life situations, blended families are better prepared to turn their challenges into chances for growth and stronger bonds.

Interactive Tools for Active Problem-Solving

In the complex world of blended family life, full of challenges and chances for growth, the interactive parts of this guide are like your navigation tools. They include practical stuff like worksheets, checklists, reflection questions, activity ideas, and access to an online community. These tools help turn the advice in this guide from just theory into something you can use daily.

Worksheets and Checklists

Worksheets and checklists aren't just more homework for families—they're essential tools in the hectic life of a blended family. Take, for example, a worksheet that helps everyone spell out their values. It's a way for everyone to write down what they believe in and hope for, making these ideas clear and actionable. Checklists for daily or weekly routines also go beyond simple task lists. They turn everyday chores into meaningful rituals, making each job an opportunity for family members to connect and strengthen their ties. Every item checked off, and every worksheet filled out isn't just another task done—it's a step towards greater unity and understanding in the family.

Reflection Questions

After each chapter, a set of reflection questions encourages readers to take a moment, look inside themselves, and connect with the material personally. These aren't just thought exercises—they're tools for gaining self-awareness and empathy. For example, when parents consider how their upbringing affects their parenting style, it can reveal hidden biases and open up ways to grow. Stepsiblings might reflect on times when they felt an unexpected bond, which helps them see the subtle connections shaping their relationship. Answering these questions gets family members thinking and talking, helping to bridge differences and deepen their understanding of the complex relationships in their blended family.

Activity Suggestions

Suggesting activities for families together brings ideas to life and turns insights into action. These activities might be as simple as cooking a meal together, where every dish has a story of heritage behind it, or as collaborative as creating a family mission statement that spells out everyone's goals and unity. Imagine spending a Sunday afternoon designing a family crest that shows off your shared values, interests, and aspirations—a symbol the whole family can rally behind. Family members create meaningful memories by doing things like this, each strengthening their sense of connection and belonging.

Online Community

Setting up an online community takes the support from this guide and brings it into a virtual space, creating a place for people dealing with blended family life to connect. This digital forum contains stories, questions, and tips, providing support and inspiration. Here, families can feel comforted knowing they're not alone. Members share their experiences like gifts, give advice generously, and celebrate each other's successes with real warmth. Although they might be far apart, everyone in this community is linked by shared experiences, forming a network alive with hope, resilience, and love.

Blended family life naturally comes with its ups and downs, and the interactive elements in this guide are like a guiding light. Worksheets and checklists help bring order, and reflection questions encourage more profound understanding and empathy. Suggested activities help strengthen connections, and the online community provides a supportive network. Together, these tools bring the ideas in this guide to life, helping blended families navigate the complexities of their lives.

Empowering Children and Teens

In a blended family, the youngest members bring unique and vibrant contributions. Their bright and resilient perspectives are crucial to the family's overall story. While adults often lead the conversations, the insights and experiences of the children and teens—covering both their struggles and victories— add depth. Listening to and actively exploring what these younger family members say is essential.

Highlighting Young Voices

Focusing on the younger members of blended families highlights their unique experiences as they navigate changes and growth. Telling their stories captures emotions from nervousness to the joy of forming new bonds. Emphasizing their perspectives provides a clear view of their challenges and successes, showcasing their resilience, flexibility, and optimism.

Empowerment Through Inclusion

Empowering the young members of a blended family means actively including them, recognizing that they're not just onlookers but key players in the family's development. Children and teens can positively impact family dynamics and contribute significantly. They can be part of making decisions that affect things like family trips and daily activities, and their viewpoints can also be crucial in resolving conflicts. Listening to what they have to say—understanding their thoughts and feelings—improves family conversations. It brings in new ideas and creates a space where everyone feels valued and heard, regardless of age.

Age-Appropriate Strategies

When involving kids and teens in discussions, decision-making, and problem-solving, it's crucial to consider their age and development level. Ensuring your approach fits their age helps them get involved and understand what's happening. For little ones, use fun, simple methods like drawing to help them express how they feel about changes in the family or use storybooks that reflect their situations to start conversations. For teens who are dealing with their own identity and independence issues, open and honest talks that treat them like the young adults they are can be more effective. This means giving them a real say in family decisions and making sure they know their opinions count. These age-appropriate methods help bridge the gap between adults and kids, making communication more effective and meaningful for everyone.

Success Stories

Amid the stories of struggles and adjustments, the success stories of kids thriving in blended families stand out, offering hope and inspiration. These real-life tales cover everything from forming close relationships with stepsiblings and stepparents to adapting to new living situations and family traditions. Each story highlights the resilience and flexibility of kids, providing comfort and valuable tips for those working through similar challenges. Sharing these stories, whether in writing, interviews, or videos, creates a supportive network, encouraging those still navigating the complex yet rewarding path of blended family life.

In the broader story of blended families, where kids' experiences often remain in the background, bringing their stories to the forefront is crucial. Focusing on their views, challenges, and achievements gives these young family members the recognition and voice they deserve. This enriches the family's overall story and emphasizes these young people's critical role in the vibrant and strong fabric of blended family life.

Expert Insights: Professional Advice and Strategies

The story of blended families is complex and often requires some outside expertise to manage its many layers effectively. This section taps into the knowledge of specialists from fields like psychology, family therapy, and financial advising. Their insights and strategies provide a strong foundation for understanding and tackling the unique challenges of blended family life, adding real depth and practical advice to help guide families.

Collaborations with Experts

Teaming up with psychologists, family therapists, and financial advisors gives us access to expert insights that help clear up the complex issues blended families face. Imagine a roundtable where experts from these fields come together, their discussions offering a range of viewpoints that help explain everything from co-parenting challenges to the financial aspects of blending families. For example, a psychologist could explain the emotional reasons behind sibling rivalry in a blended family and offer empathy-based strategies to handle it. Meanwhile, a family therapist might suggest ways to improve communication between stepparents and stepchildren to strengthen their relationships. And a financial advisor could help sort out how to combine household finances, providing specific tips on budgeting and saving that work well for blended families. This team approach expands the range of solutions and ensures the advice is solid from experienced professionals.

Evidence-Based Approaches

The real value of any advice lies in its solid, research-backed foundation, especially when it comes to blended families. The methods and strategies suggested here are based on research and studies that prove their effectiveness, not just guesses or theories. For example, the idea of holding regular family meetings to improve communication comes from research showing it can help strengthen family ties and solve conflicts better. Also, the advice on combining different parenting styles is backed by studies that show how consistency and teamwork in parenting can positively affect children's well-being. This way, the advice goes beyond personal stories and offers families a proven and reliable guide.

Professional Tips and Tricks

Beyond the broad strokes of strategy and approach, the nuances of navigating blended family life often lie in the details. Here, professionals offer tips and tricks, nuggets of wisdom honed through years of practice. These may include practical exercises for building empathy between stepsiblings, communication templates for discussing sensitive topics with ex-partners, or financial worksheets to facilitate transparent discussions about money. Each tip is a tool to navigate the specific challenges blended families encounter. For example, a therapist might suggest a "feelings jar" where family members can deposit notes about their emotions, facilitating discussions in a non-confrontational manner. A financial advisor, on the other hand, might recommend apps that help track expenses and manage budgets collaboratively, addressing the logistical challenges of merging household finances.

Resource Directory

Navigating blended family life, with all its challenges and rewards, is something families have to do with others. A detailed directory of resources acts like a guide, pointing families to helpful books, websites, and professional services. This directory covers various topics, from legal advice on stepparent adoption to forums for stepchildren looking for others in similar situations. Each listing includes a brief description, making it easy for families to find what matches their specific needs. Whether it's a book diving into the psychology of blended families, a website with co-parenting plan templates, or therapists specializing in blended family issues, this directory ensures families have a strong support network at their fingertips.

This section helps blended families find their way by gathering advice and strategies from various experts. It combines professional insights, evidence-based practices, valuable tips, and a comprehensive resource list, giving families the tools to manage their unique situations effectively. This well-rounded approach means that the story of blended families isn't just about the problems they face but also about the solutions they find and the successes they achieve, all supported by experts committed to helping these families thrive.

Blended Family Successes: Inspirational Stories

In the complex world of blended families, moments of triumph stand out, showing the harmony that comes from patience, understanding, and love. These stories, full of challenges and victories, highlight these families' resilience. They serve as powerful examples for others still figuring out the dynamics of their new family lives.

Inspirational Narratives

Success stories in blended families often start in simple moments that bloom into real unity and joy. Take, for instance, a family that struggled with different discipline and communication styles but found common ground by cooking meals together every week. Initiated by a stepparent wanting to connect, this cooking ritual became a treasured tradition filled with laughter and shared recipes, bringing everyone closer with every meal they made. Another story comes from a teenager who was initially wary of the changes a parent's remarriage brought but found a true friend in a stepsibling, leading to a relationship built on mutual respect and deep affection. These real-life tales highlight how openness, empathy, and a readiness to accept change can truly transform blended family life.

Diversity of Successes

Success in blended families looks different for everyone; it comes in many forms and happens in various ways. For some, it's about combining holiday traditions in a way that respects everyone's background while also bringing the family together. For others, it might be the small, quiet moments of connection between a stepparent and stepchild—these little instances can mean a lot, showing deep acceptance and love. This variety shows that success in blended families isn't about eliminating the differences but blending them into a united, beautiful family life.

Lessons Learned

Every success story from blended families brings helpful lessons that others can apply. One key lesson is keeping communication open, a common thread in stories where families moved past initial misunderstandings to form a united front. Another critical point is the creation of shared experiences, like traveling, enjoying hobbies, or establishing daily routines together, all of which help strengthen connections and build understanding. Patience and building relationships, especially between stepparents and stepchildren, are crucial for developing trust and affection. These lessons, drawn from real-life experiences, act as signposts, helping guide other blended families to find harmony and happiness.

Celebration Ideas

Recognizing and celebrating milestones and successes is vital to strengthening the positive vibes in blended families. There are many ways to celebrate, from simple acts to grand gestures, each reflecting the family's journey and achievements. For example, setting up a Family Achievement Wall with photos, notes, and keepsakes helps visually remind everyone how far they've come together. Or, hosting a Blended Family Day filled with activities that cater to everyone's interests and backgrounds can be a fun and inclusive way to celebrate. Even sharing stories of personal successes during a family dinner or around a campfire can become a meaningful tradition that strengthens the family bond.

In conclusion, the stories, lessons, and celebrations of blended family life create a rich and complex mix of experiences. By sharing inspiring stories, recognizing the different forms success can take, learning valuable lessons, and embracing celebrations, blended families can find guidance toward their moments of success. As we explore more strategies and insights, let's remember that success in blended families isn't just about overcoming challenges but also celebrating these unique family connections' beauty, diversity, and strength.

ELEVEN

Nurturing Hope and Resilience in Blended Families

In the middle of a thick forest, it's hard for sunlight to get through the dense tree cover. But when a single ray of light breaks through, it can change the scene below, bringing warmth and encouraging growth in places that were once shadows. Blended families are a lot like this forest. They face many challenges and complexities but hope acts like that beam of sunlight—lighting the way, warming hearts, and helping growth in even the most challenging spots.

Hope as a Foundation

Hope is a powerful force that helps blended families look past their immediate challenges. It encourages them to focus on better days ahead, even when current circumstances seem tough. Take, for example, planting a garden in a new home. It's a simple act, but it means a lot—it shows a commitment to the future and growing together as a family. Like the family, the garden symbolizes hope, growing and thriving through the seasons. Each seed planted is a step forward, a problem solved, and a relationship strengthened. The intertwined roots of the garden reflect how each family member contributes to the well-being of the whole group.

Stories of Hope

Real-life stories from blended families who have overcome early challenges to find harmony and joy are incredibly inspiring. These stories, often shared on family blogs, social media, or community forums, are powerful examples of what hope and perseverance can achieve. For instance, a family might talk about their tradition of planting a tree for each significant milestone, symbolizing the growth of their unity and love. These authentic, emotional stories highlighted the crucial moments when hope helped them push through tough times, showcasing the big difference that sticking together and staying positive can make.

Maintaining Hope

Keeping hope alive during tough times takes deliberate effort and changes in seeing things. One way to do this is by keeping a family gratitude journal. Writing down small daily wins and happy moments can shift the focus from what's missing to what's going well, from problems to successes. Also, spending some time creating family vision boards can be motivating. When everyone can express their hopes and dreams for the family visually, it helps point everyone in the same direction. This fun activity brings the family closer and strengthens the connections between everyone.

Hope and Resilience

In blended families, hope and resilience work together in a powerful cycle—hope boosts resilience, and resilience strengthens hope. Workshops to build resilience, often run by community centers or family therapists, can help families. These workshops equip everyone with practical ways to adapt, bounce back, and grow from tough times. Through role-playing, stress management exercises, and open discussions, families learn that resilience isn't just something you're born with; it's a skill that can be developed with practice and support. As families get better at handling challenges resiliently, their hope for a happier, more united future grows stronger, laying the groundwork for lasting success and joy.

Visual Element: The Family Resilience Tree

Adding something like a Family Resilience Tree provides a clear picture of a blended family's growth and unity as they overcome challenges. In this activity, you create a giant tree poster where the roots stand for the family's core values, the trunk represents the support system, and the branches and leaves show each person's hopes, dreams, and successes. Families can add new elements to their tree during key milestones or reflective moments, visually tracking their progress and resilience. This fun and thoughtful activity reminds everyone of their journey and strength and sparks deeper conversations and connections among family members.

In the journey of blending lives, where challenges seem overwhelming, hope acts like a guiding light, leading families to warmth, growth, and togetherness. Blended families can find their way by sharing success stories, practicing gratitude, building resilience, and creating visual symbols like the resilience tree. Like a carefully tended garden, the path of a blended family, rooted in hope and resilience, is filled with potential for beauty, shared happiness, and strong relationships.

From Surviving to Thriving: Enhancing Family Dynamics

In blended families, life can often feel like a play full of tension, misunderstandings, and the shadows of past relationships. But within these complex situations, there's a vast potential for growth and change. Moving from just getting by to genuinely thriving together requires patience, perseverance, and a mindset focused on growth. This approach views each challenge not as a barrier but as a chance to strengthen bonds and build closer family ties. It's fertile ground for nurturing understanding, empathy, and resilience, turning difficulties into opportunities for everyone to grow together.

Embracing this mindset means changing how we handle problems, focusing more on long-term possibilities than short-term conflicts. Take, for example, the blending of different family traditions. Instead of clashing over differences, this can be a chance for creativity and teamwork. Families can come together to create new traditions that blend everyone's backgrounds, making a rich new culture uniquely theirs. This process isn't just about compromise; it's a symbol of the family's ability to adapt and grow, showing how they move from being a group of individuals to a tight-knit unit.

Practical Transformation Strategies

Transforming family dynamics takes more than just changing your outlook; it requires practical steps that turn good intentions into tangible actions. These steps act like building blocks, helping the family shape its new identity. For example, holding regular family meetings provides a structured way to talk things out, celebrate wins, and solve problems together. Making this a regular part of family life boosts openness, ensures everyone is heard, and builds a culture of respect and teamwork.

Also, working together on shared projects like starting a family garden, volunteering, or putting together a family cookbook can bring everyone together. These activities are not just about the result but about working together, strengthening the family's bond and giving everyone a sense of achievement and shared purpose. This shows how working together can transform family life and bring everyone closer.

Empowering Families

True transformation in a blended family goes beyond just using new strategies; it's about empowering every family member to shape the family's future actively. This empowerment touches everything—emotions, practical skills, and relationships. Emotionally, it creates a space where everyone can share their feelings and concerns without fear of judgment. Practically, it involves giving everyone the tools and skills they need to handle the unique challenges of blended family life, like communication techniques and ways to solve conflicts. On a relational level, it's about recognizing and appreciating each person's unique role in the family, making sure everyone, from the kids to the adults, feels valued and heard.

When everyone feels empowered, the family can do more than just get by; they can thrive. They start to see the challenges and complexities as obstacles and opportunities to grow stronger and more united.

Celebrating Transformation

The transformation in family dynamics calls for a celebration. But this isn't just about hitting traditional milestones; it's more about recognizing the journey itself—the challenges faced and the strong connections forged along the way. It's a time to reflect, pause and appreciate all the effort, growth, and deepened love that's come out of this process. Whether it's a special family ritual on the anniversary of becoming a blended family or just taking a moment to acknowledge overcoming a tough challenge, these celebrations mark critical points in the family's story. They remind everyone of their resilience and ability to grow and thrive, no matter how tangled things initially seem.

Moving from just getting by to genuinely thriving, blended families go through a tough and rewarding journey. Developing a growth mindset, implementing practical transformation strategies, empowering each family member to shape their collective future and celebrating critical moments is crucial. With these efforts, the family becomes stronger, more united, and better because of its challenges. In this new state, a blended family is a powerful example of how love, resilience, and a steadfast belief in growth and renewal can bring out the best in everyone.

Implementing Change: Steps for Immediate Results

Making changes, like looking up at a giant fog-covered mountain, can be daunting. It's easy to feel unsure and a bit scared about starting. But remember, there's already a path laid out by those who've gone before us, showing that it's doable. Change doesn't need to start with massive, sweeping actions. It's more about making small, deliberate steps. Think of it like laying bricks—one at a time—each one gradually building towards a more harmonious family life.

Immediate Action Plan

At the core of any significant change is a clear roadmap that outlines precisely what needs to be done to get there. This plan is about practicality, breaking down the transformation into doable tasks that gradually move the family toward its goals. For example, setting up a weekly family meeting where everyone gets a chance to speak and be heard can be a vital part of this plan—it's where understanding and empathy start to grow from sharing thoughts and feelings. Another helpful tool can be a shared family calendar. It might seem simple, but keeping everyone's schedules aligned is crucial so that time together isn't lost in the daily rush. No matter how small, each task is packed with purpose, each acting like a piece in the change puzzle.

Small Changes, Big Impact

The transformation within blended families often comes from small changes, those little tweaks that can shift everyday life, changing how things feel and work. Something as straightforward as rearranging the living space to better represent everyone's lives and stories can make a difference. It shows, in a visible way, the unity and inclusiveness the family aims for. Similarly, starting a family hobby or project, like gardening or making art together, helps blend everyone's contributions into a collective story, building a sense of belonging and shared identity. These minor adjustments, each adding a little more to the picture, gradually combine to create a harmonious family life—proof that small steps can lead to significant changes.

Tracking Progress

The journey toward change can be unpredictable, so having markers to track progress is helpful. A family progress journal can serve this purpose, offering a tangible record of milestones achieved, challenges faced, and lessons learned. Each member can add reflections, creating a mosaic of perspectives showing the family's evolution. This journal provides a historical account of the journey and acts as a mirror, reflecting the growth that often goes unnoticed daily. Reviewing this journal during family meetings turns it into a meaningful ritual, allowing everyone to pause, appreciate their progress, and renew their commitment to moving forward together.

Adjusting Strategies

Family life can be unpredictable, so it's important to have a flexible plan. Understanding that things don't always go as planned allows for adjustments when circumstances change. This might mean reassessing roles and responsibilities, realigning expectations, or introducing new communication techniques to address emerging challenges. Open dialogue is key, where feedback is welcomed, and the willingness to adapt is seen as a strategic move toward harmony. Based on the family's experiences, this ongoing adjustment ensures that strategies remain relevant and effective.

In blended families, initiating and maintaining change requires practical action, reflection, and adjustment. It's about taking meaningful steps toward unity and understanding. The action plan serves as the guide, small changes are the milestones, tracking progress is the compass, and adjusting strategies is the rudder, steering the family toward harmonious coexistence.

Strengthening Family Connections

The bonds that hold blended families together go beyond shared spaces and last names. They rely on trust, understanding, and mutual respect. These connections form a strong foundation that can withstand daily challenges. Building these bonds requires a deliberate approach, using communication tools, spending quality time together, and respecting each other.

Strengthening Relationships

Building strong family bonds relies on trust and understanding, essential for any household. This is especially important in blended families, where listening is as critical as speaking. Something as simple as a weekly Listening Circle can change the family dynamic. In a quiet and dedicated space, each family member takes turns sharing their thoughts, feelings and needs while everyone else listens attentively. This practice helps ensure everyone feels heard and valued, fostering a sense of safety and belonging. These moments of shared vulnerability help build trust and create lasting connections.

Communication as a Tool

If trust is the foundation, communication is the framework that keeps a blended family together. Family members navigate their shared lives through talking and listening, avoiding misunderstandings and conflicts. Improving communication skills takes practice and patience; family communication workshops can significantly help. These workshops, led by skilled facilitators, teach participants to express themselves clearly and listen empathetically. They focus on techniques like using "I" statements to express personal feelings without blaming others and reflective listening to ensure messages are understood correctly. Through role-playing everyday scenarios, families learn how to communicate in ways that strengthen their relationships.

Quality Time

In the busyness of daily routines, quality time often gets pushed aside by work, school, and chores. But it's during these moments of togetherness that family life truly happens. Creating these moments means intentionally stepping away from the busyness and setting aside time for family interactions. A monthly hike or a family book club can bring everyone together. These activities provide fun, strengthen family bonds, and create lasting memories.

Respecting Individual Relationships

In a blended family, each relationship has its unique dynamics and importance. Whether the bond between a stepparent and stepchild or between siblings and half-siblings, each connection brings challenges and rewards. It's crucial to nurture these individual relationships for the family to thrive. This can mean setting aside special time for one-on-one interactions tailored to each relationship.

For example, a stepfather and stepdaughter might share a love for astronomy, using stargazing to connect and communicate. Siblings might work on a project that reflects their shared heritage, strengthening their bond. By honoring and nurturing these individual relationships, the family builds a stronger, more connected unit where each bond is valued.

Building strong bonds in a blended family takes patience, practice, and a focus on trust, communication, shared experiences, and respect. These actions help bring everyone together, creating a close, lasting family connection.

Looking to the Future: Growing Together as a Blended Family

Creating a blended family involves envisioning a shared future, a critical step. It's about bringing together everyone's dreams and goals to guide decisions and shape the family's path. This shared vision lays the foundation for a future filled with love, understanding, and mutual support.

Crafting this vision starts with including everyone's dreams through open discussions. Each family member contributes, painting a picture of their future together. Whether traveling, home buying, or community involvement, each goal reflects the family's united purpose and direction.

Life changes, and families need to adapt. Communication, boundaries, and support must also change as children grow and roles evolve. The teen years, for example, may require new approaches to maintaining balance. Adapting ensures that family bonds remain strong and harmonious over time.

The blended family's journey aims to create a lasting legacy of love and understanding. This legacy is built through compassion, resilience, mutual respect, shared stories, traditions, and everyday acts of empathy. It's a gift for future generations, guiding them with love and unity.

Recognizing that the journey is continuous and filled with challenges and triumphs is a source of strength. The path is not linear but a winding road with moments of connection and growth. Challenges offer opportunities for deeper bonds, and triumphs celebrate the family's progress. Embracing this journey helps the blended family discover the depth of their connection, defined by their collective resilience, love, and shared vision.

Conclusion

As we reach the end of this book, let's reflect on the incredible journey of blended families. We've explored families' complex yet rewarding path, facing challenges like establishing new dynamics, navigating financial planning, and fostering strong relationships. It's a journey that requires immense resilience and love to turn these obstacles into opportunities for growth and deeper connections.

Throughout this book, we've emphasized the importance of hope and adaptability. These themes are essential in maintaining a positive outlook and a harmonious family life, even when the road gets tough. Remember, the ability to adapt and stay hopeful can pave the way for a fulfilling family experience.

Now, it's time for action. Strengthening family bonds requires ongoing effort. Regularly revisit the strategies we've discussed, keep communication open and honest, and commit to continuous learning and adaptation as your family evolves.

Engage with the broader blended family community. Sharing your experiences, challenges, and successes with others on the same journey can be incredibly valuable. This connection helps you realize you're not alone and offers support from those who truly understand your situation.

This book is more than just a guide; it's a companion on your journey. Return to it as a resource during different stages of your family's development, from the initial blending to navigating the teenage years and beyond. Let it support you through every twist and turn.

I want to leave you with a message of hope and celebration. With patience, understanding, and love, blended families can thrive. Celebrate the unique joy and richness of bringing diverse individuals together to form a united, loving family.

Remember, the essence of a blended family lies not in its challenges but in the incredible opportunity it presents for growth, love, and lasting bonds. Embrace your journey with open hearts and minds, and build a legacy of love and understanding for future generations.

Keeping the Game Alive

Now that you have everything you need to build a strong, united, blended family, it's time to pass on your new knowledge and show other readers where they can find the same help.

Leaving your honest opinion of this book on Amazon will show other blended families where they can find the guidance they're looking for and help them navigate their unique journeys.

Let's keep the game alive, passing on the torch of knowledge and igniting the hopes of future blended families. Your role in this journey is crucial, and I am profoundly grateful for your help in making the *Comprehensive Guide to Blended Family Success* accessible and helpful for all.

Here's to continuing our journey with new knowledge and a shared purpose. Thank you for being an essential part of this adventure.

To leave a review, just scan the QR code below:

References

"5 Exercises to Help You Build More Empathy." 2021. *Ideas.Ted.Com* (blog). March 16, 2021. https://ideas.ted.com/5-exercises-to-help-you-build-more-empathy/.

"6 Steps for Successful Family Goal Setting." 2020. Spero Financial. 2020. https://spero.financial/6-steps-for-successful-family-goal-setting/.

Admin, Eagle Family. "The Role of Step Parents in Christian Blended Families." Eagle Family Ministries, September 8, 2023. https://www.eaglefamily.org/the-role-of-stepparents-in-christian-blended-families/.

"Best Co-Parenting Communication Tools for Child Custody." 2023. Talking Parents. Monitored Communications, LLC. 2023. https://talkingparents.com/home.

Blended Families and Navigating Through FAFSA | Stock, Carlson & Asso. LLC. "Blended Families and Navigating Through FAFSA | Stock, Carlson & Asso. LLC." Accessed April 12, 2024. https://www.dupagelawyers.com/wheaton-family-law-estate-planning/blended-families-navigating-fafsa.

"Blended Family and Step-Parenting Tips - HelpGuide.Org." 2019. Https://Www.Helpguide.Org. 2024 2019. https://www.helpguide.org/articles/parenting-family/step-parenting-blended-families.htm.

Campbell, Richard. "Parental Involvement in Game-Based Learning: 5 Strategies," September 30, 2023. https://richardccampbell.com/parental-involvement-in-game-based-learning/.

Carnelley, Katherine, and Gregory Maio. 2008. "Unraveling the Role of Forgiveness in Family Relationships." *Journal of Personality and Social Psychology* 94 (2): 307–19.

"Co-Parenting and Joint Custody Tips for Divorced Parents." n.d. Https://Www.Helpguide.Org. https://www.helpguide.org/articles/parenting-family/co-parenting-tips-for-divorced-parents.htm.

"Co-Parenting Conflict Resolution Techniques | OurFamilyWizard." Accessed April 12, 2024. https://www.ourfamilywizard.com/blog/co-parenting-conflict-resolution-techniques.

"Creating a Perfect Parenting Plan in 6 Steps | OurFamilyWizard." Accessed April 12, 2024. https://www.ourfamilywizard.com/blog/creating-perfect-parenting-plan-6-steps.

Cunningham, Lori. "Estate Planning for Blended Families: Pitfalls and Solutions." *CunninghamLegal* (blog), March 10, 2021. https://www.cunninghamlegal.com/estate-planning-for-blended-families-pitfalls-and-solutions/.

"Estate Planning for Blended Families: Complete Guide | Farm Bureau Financial Services." Accessed April 12, 2024. https://www.fbfs.com/learning-center/estate-planning-for-blended-families.

"Estate Strategies: Conducting a Family Meeting About Finances." 2019. Benjamin F.

Edwards & Co. Investments for Generations. https://benjaminfedwards.com/wp-content/uploads/2017/09/Conducting-a-Family-Meeting-About-Finances.pdf.

Extension. "10 Tips for Successful Family Meetings - 10.249." Accessed April 12, 2024. https://extension.colostate.edu/topic-areas/family-home-consumer/10-tips-for-successful-family-meetings/.

Fletcher, R. "Positive Discipline Methods for Children." Military OneSource, June 2, 2021. https://www.militaryonesource.mil/parenting/new-parents/tips-for-disciplining-your-child/.

Gaspard, Terry. "Managing Conflict in Blended Families." The Gottman Institute, January 23, 2023. https://www.gottman.com/blog/managing-conflict-in-blended-families/.

Guidance, The Family, and Therapy Center. "Open Communication in a Blended Family | Family Guidance & Therapy Center," February 28, 2020. https://familyguidanceandtherapy.com/open-communication-in-a-blended-family/.

"How to Communicate Effectively with Your Young Child | UNICEF Parenting." Accessed April 12, 2024. https://www.unicef.org/parenting/child-care/9-tips-for-better-communication.

"How to Promote Inclusion in Blended Families – International Nanny Association." Accessed April 12, 2024. https://nanny.org/how-to-promote-inclusion-in-blended-families/.

"How to Write a Family Mission Statement (With Examples)." 2023. wikiHow. 2023. https://www.wikihow.com/Family-Mission-Statement.

King, Valarie, Lisa M. Boyd, and Maggie L. Thorsen. "Adolescents' Perceptions of Family Belonging in Stepfamilies." *Journal of Marriage and the Family* 77, no. 3 (June 1, 2015): 761–74. https://doi.org/10.1111/jomf.12181.

LCSW, Amber Johnson, MSW. "3 Tips for Parenting as a United Front." *North Shore Family Services* (blog), December 3, 2019. https://northshorefamilyservices.com/3-tips-for-parenting-as-a-united-front/.

M, Prapoorna. "The Role of Self-Care in Maintaining Healthy Relationships." *WellnessHub* (blog), February 29, 2024. https://www.mywellnesshub.in/blog/the-role-of-self-care-in-maintaining-healthy-relationships/.

Mixed Up Mama. "The Secrets to Making Your Multicultural Family Work." *Mixed Up Mama* (blog), April 9, 2019. https://mixedracefamily.com/secrets-multicultural-family-work/.

McKinley Irvin. "Common Legal Challenges Blended Families Face During the Divorce Process." Accessed April 12, 2024. https://www.mckinleyirvin.com/family-law-blog/2023/september/common-legal-challenges-blended-families-face-du/.

ParentMap. "5 Questions That Turn Challenges Into Growth Opportunities for Kids." Accessed April 12, 2024. https://www.parentmap.com/parenting-challenges-growth-opportunities.

Paulus, Nathan. "Financial Planning for Blended Families." MoneyGeek.com, August 31, 2023. https://www.moneygeek.com/financial-planning/resources/blended-family-finances/.

Ph.D, Jeremy Sutton. "Conflict Resolution in Relationships & Couples: 5 Strategies." PositivePsychology.com, November 9, 2021. https://positivepsychology.com/conflict-resolution-relationships/.

Portrie, Torey, and Nicole R. Hill. "Blended Families: A Critical Review of the Current Research." *The Family Journal* 13, no. 4 (October 2005): 445–51. https://doi.org/10.1177/1066480705279014.

Project Management for Parents. "15 Ideas for Family Team Building." Accessed April 12, 2024. https://www.projectmanagementforparents.com/blog/15-ideas-for-family-team-building.

State (militaryfamilies.psu.edu), Clearinghouse for Military Family Readiness at Penn. "Holidays with a Blended Family: 10 Tips for Parents and Stepparents." Thrive, December 1, 2023. https://thrive.psu.edu/blog/holidays-with-a-blended-family-10-tips-for-parents-and-stepparents/.

The Center for Family Unity. "Three Tips for Understanding and Avoiding Loyalty Conflicts," June 13, 2015. http://www.thecenterforfamilyunity.com/three-tips-for-understanding-and-avoiding-loyalty-conflicts/.

"The Challenges of Stepparenting | Psychology Today." Accessed April 12, 2024. https://www.psychologytoday.com/us/blog/fixing-families/202103/the-challenges-stepparenting.

Together, Mary Leigh @ Live Well Play. "25 Awesome Date Night Ideas for Busy Parents." *Live Well Play Together* (blog), February 11, 2019. https://www.livewellplaytogether.com/25-awesome-date-night-ideas-for-busy-parents/.

University, Utah State. "How to Merge Traditions, Celebrations and Milestones in A Stepfamily." Accessed April 12, 2024. https://extension.usu.edu/hru/blog/how-to-merge-traditions-celebrations-and-milestones-in-a-stepfamily.

US News & World Report. "5 Ways to Promote Harmony in Blended Families." Accessed April 12, 2024. https://health.usnews.com/wellness/for-parents/articles/2017-05-02/5-ways-to-promote-harmony-in-blended-families.

Verywell Mind. "7 Active Listening Techniques to Practice in Your Daily Conversations." Accessed April 12, 2024. https://www.verywellmind.com/what-is-active-listening-3024343.

www.ingramcontent.com/pod-product-compliance
Lightning Source LLC
LaVergne TN
LVHW051838080426
835512LV00018B/2954